Hitting Our Stride

Women, Work and What Matters

Karel Murray

Building a Better You One Story at a Time

Hitting Our Stride: Women, Work, and What Matters: Building Self-Confidence through Advice and Mentoring for Women and their Issues

Karel Murray
2731 Ragley Drive
Waterloo, Iowa 50701
(866) 817-2986

E-Mail: karel@karel.com
Main Web Site: http://www.Karel.com
Podcast Web Site: http://www.JustForAMomentPodcast.com
Book Web Site: http://www.HittingOurStride.net

Limits of Liability and Disclaimer of Warranty
The author and publisher shall not be liable for your misuse of this material. This book is strictly for informational and educational purposes.

Warning—Disclaimer
The purpose of this book is to educate and entertain. The author and/or publisher do not guarantee that anyone following these techniques, suggestions, tips, ideas, or strategies will engender success. The author and/or publisher shall have neither liability nor responsibility to anyone with respect to any loss or damage caused, or alleged to be caused, directly or indirectly by the information contained in this book.

ISBN: 978-0-9822015-4-1 (paperback)

Printed in the United States   Cover & Interior Design by:
                                        Ronda Taylor

Roberts & Ross Publishing
Englewood, Colorado
(303) 762-1469
Santa Rosa Beach, Florida
(850) 622-5772

www.RobertsRossPublishing.com

What business leaders and professionals have to say about working with Karel Murray:

"Karel has the unique ability to 1) listen to what the client wants, 2) structure a program to meet those needs in an informative and fun way, and 3) engage her participants. Karel Murray is excellent and I would recommend her to anyone who wants to improve their organization."
~ Susan Kubiesa, Vice President, Zurich Commercial, Chicago, IL

"Karel is one of the most engaging and energizing speakers I've seen. She is brilliant at using humor to convey her messages. She has the ability to make everyone in the room feel like she is talking to THEM! I know that everyone I spoke to thought Karel is wonderful and relates on either a personal or professional level to the topics she presents."
~ Rosalyn Lorenz, President, Cedar Falls Business & Professional Women

"Karel has a unique gift in her approach, sharing life stories and reminding us all that we take life's situations too seriously. She gave us the insight to value our "circumstances" rather than perceiving ourselves as victims. Great speaker, excellent presentation."
~ Christie Milligan, Skiff Medical Center

"Karel is an outstanding speaker. She has a great way of blending humor with giving a serious message. She was the best keynote we have ever had!"
~ Theresa Beem, Buena Vista Regional Medical Center

"With humor, enthusiasm and storytelling, Karel tells you to accept who you are and to follow your dreams. She is a great role model for women."
~ Deb Kougias, AVP Mount Vernon Bank and Trust

"Karel talks about life and how you can overcome it. Whatever you want out of life, go for it!"

~ Diane Chumbley

"So many things Karel said are mirrored in my own life. I know now that I can't wait for others to make me happy—that's my responsibility."

~ Sandra Jirele, Express Personnel

"I was touched by how she shared personal stories, including painfully poignant ones. I admire her courage to be a strong and emotional woman. What a wonderful role model for women today."

~ Julie Baysen

"Karel touched my heart, my soul. She shared with us deeply, truly, and with humor and deep emotion. She showed us that you can play the game without forsaking your integrity."

~ Rebecca Darrington

"Karel's humor during some of life's disappointing moments was very inspiring."

~ Claudia Mefford

"She is a great example of overcoming obstacles and keeping your values and integrity."

~ Barbara Stowe

"Karel is an outstanding speaker. She made us laugh, brought us to tears and back to laughter. She made us feel good about ourselves and the jobs we do. Karel is very professional and puts you at ease the moment you meet her."

~ Vickie McVey, School Nutrition Association of Iowa

Contents

Introduction

If you were to stop right now and reflect upon your life, what lessons come to mind? Did the impact of those lessons make you want to curl up in a fetal ball or did they bring out your inner lioness? As you continue to struggle to figure out what your contribution will be to your corner of the world, do you tend to get lost in the details of day-to-day survival, feeling like you're stuck in a maze and can't quite figure out the right direction?

These questions and more bombarded me for most of my life until I finally understood I wasn't alone. I've always been fiercely independent my whole life, but I have come to appreciate the importance of my female friends and peers. Together women have a collective strength and wisdom, and we shouldn't be keeping it to ourselves!

Because of what I do—speaking to groups about personal accountability and self-esteem—I'm constantly in touch with women in their 40s and 50s. I'm always amazed at what these women have to bring to the table. Think about it. Some of us were born right in the middle of 1950s, June-Cleaveresque conformity. But it was also the calm before the storm, for we were on the verge of the next wave of the feminist revolution—a bra-burning, flag-waving march on our collective idea of what women do (a revolution that others of you were impacted by being born to the generation that was causing this change). We Baby-boomer women, for better or worse, were brought up in conflict—old values versus new. Do women leave the home and help provide for their families? What does it mean for a woman to work in a man's world? What does it mean for the kids when their moms aren't home to be all at once chef, maid, referee, and soft-shoulder for the little ones?

For the younger generation of females, these questions are absurd. The revolution was won. The younger generations don't feel the hardness of the glass ceiling that we've grown so accustomed to—the one that we don't even see getting thinner and thinner. To them, it's a no-brainer. Of course they're going to have a career and a family, and they don't think twice about how they're going to balance it—even though they still need help with that acrobatic act.

We're entering a new phase of our lives—we've either gone through or are fast approaching our "change," that very interesting euphemism for menopause. Now our body is conducting its own revolution and reminding us that change comes whether we like it or not. But here's the good news. With this shift, both physically and mentally, we're now just hitting our stride. We're coming into our own, realizing our power, and understanding all that we have to give to each other and to the up and coming females who want to follow in our intrepid footsteps.

And that's what this book is all about. I wanted to gather the collective wisdom of my fellow woman. I wanted to find out from females what they thought about where they have been and offer advice to live comfortably with ourselves in the up-and-coming years. So this is what I did. I surveyed a bunch of women on all sorts of questions we, as females, often ponder about life, love, work and family. (I'll list them a bit further down in this introduction). Why? I realized together we can create an opportunity to clarify our vision for the next phase of our lives and reach for our individual milestones.

I also found out that the force of shared wisdom and collaboration is unbeatable when combined with a commitment to gather up our collective skirts and dare to live joyously.

Validation from other women can provide us with a safe haven of sorts. The 168 women who responded provided varying points of view on life's questions; at times some of the answers proved to be almost too painful to read while others practically lift off the page in emotional buoyancy.

By sharing this information with you, my hope is that you will stop, take a deep breath, and then face the traps you might have set in your own mind, address problems you have put on yourself, and conquer issues that assault you from outside influences.

For me, that deep breath of reflection came when I visited my dying mother. In a way, that day was the genesis of this book.

On her porch, overlooking a park full of oak trees in their full autumn colorful glory, my mother rocked quietly in her lawn chair. A cup of over brewed coffee nestled in her strong hands; she looked as peaceful as I've ever seen her. Expressionless, she observed two squirrels chasing each other across the overgrown yard, chattering as they raced up and down tree trunks.

"People are like that." Without looking at me, she acknowledged my presence. "They race after whatever they feel is important and don't ever seem to stop to take a breath. I miss that."

She turned her head toward me and that's when I saw defeat written in her eyes...something I'd never witnessed before. My mother had given up.

For God's sake, who could blame her? Multiple rounds of chemotherapy, which physically incapacitated her and left a ravaged hairless body; this proud elderly woman was reduced to a walker and unable to manage even the simplest things. She knew the consequences of ovarian cancer, acknowledged that she had lost the ability to think clearly, and yet her inability to release control created an inner turmoil.

That day, my mother began revealing her life by unraveling mysteries and clarifying perspectives for me. At forty, I finally no longer saw her as my mother but as a woman who had endured what all women endure. This strong willed, aggressive woman shared stories that made me laugh and swallow a sob. She didn't want pity; she urged me to understand that she had made choices in her life that had outcomes she didn't expect but had to live with anyway.

The gift my mother gave me before she passed away in August 2007 was an understanding of what shaped my childhood and life perspective. She forced me to realize that I am ultimately the only person who can determine how my life will unfold.

I guess that ruins the concept that life just happens…

No more blaming my parents for all of my deficiencies, no more ranting about how things don't seem to go as planned when I read about young millionaires in *Entrepreneur* magazine. I'm supposed to be in control of what happens to me?

It isn't fair.

Sometimes I want to blame someone or something else for my choices. It makes me feel better. I need to be able to reflect about my situation and say there's a grand scheme for my life that is beyond my control. I think the words I'm looking for are "personal accountability." For example, this quote says it all:

"In our choices, lies our fate."
Guillermo del Tora, Hollywood director

And this is exactly what scares the daylights out of me. All of us have our priorities. No one else sets them for us—we do. We either say *yes!* to a choice or we set it aside. My fear is that I'll say *yes* for all the right reasons, yet find out later that decision set in motion another entirely separate chain of events. Are we really in control or is what happens to us random? Do we waste time covering old ground or spend it surging forward with a new understanding?

Listening to my mom that day, I realized I've spent much of my life keeping things isolated within my own heart. And If I do that, do others? Is that why many people fall prey to destructive behavior so they don't have to look too deeply inside themselves? How tragic of us to not share with each other. How sad, in a way, that I only began to see my mother as a woman, not just as a mom, as she was dying.

It made me wonder. Perhaps accountability for our actions is a burden too heavy to bear for some. The "what ifs" and "if onlys" become a convenient place to park our emotions, just taking a breather until we figure out the next step. But, in reality, those next steps are so vital. They're going to move us into some of the best years of our lives!

I'm working hard to break my isolation because I understand now how personal accountability is directly related to cause and effect. I say something harsh to someone, should I be surprised when they respond in the same manner? If I ignore my child to watch my favorite program, should I be startled when they think I never listen to them? If I eat ice cream every day, why should I be surprised I gained weight?

When will I learn that I'm responsible for my own predicament? How do people keep getting up and putting on a brave face for the world? I know my past challenges have shaped me into the person I am today. I don't get any "redos." Could my life have taken a different direction and would I be as happy as I am today? Who knows? That's the disturbing part of making choices. We will never know where the other path might have guided us. I think that is why we like movies like "*Ground Hog Day*" with Bill Murray where he keeps living the same day over and over again until he gets it right.

But that only happens in movies, in life there are no do-overs. However, that doesn't mean that we can't plan for those next steps. As we hit our stride ladies, I think it's important that we take the time to reflect on the choices we have made and the people we admire. Let's collect our experiences to provide others the opportunity of a glimpse into their possible future. This is what I hope to achieve with this book.

The 168 women who responded to my survey answered questions that included feedback on such things as self-image, what they had learned from their parents, the fears they secretly harbor and advice to other females. I wanted to get real responses to issues that strong, smart women faced, sometimes daily.

These are the questions I asked and the reason why I felt it was important to ask:

- *What is your greatest personal strength?*

    Women in my generation have had to master a number of skills in order to compete on the corporate battlefield. Typically women are noted for intuition, empathy and a service attitude. Today, do we appreciate other characteristics that are more success driven?

- *What is your greatest personal fear? What scares you the most?*

  Fear can cripple a person's ability be proactive in making change, therefore I asked this question to explore what women dread and to look for trends in attitudes.

- *How do you feel about the world we live in today using a few defining words?*

  I conduct ethics courses nationwide and a frequent refrain centers on the general lack of character, integrity, and ethical behavior. I wondered if this group thought in terms of a glass half full or half empty.

- *What lessons did you learn from your mother? What lessons did you learn from your father?*

  Children bond uniquely with each parent, and I wanted to know what different lessons were gleaned as a result.

- *What did you learn about life by observing your parents?*

  It's one thing to be taught specific rules and appropriate behavior, but what "silent" message actually impacted the women who answered this survey; are we shaped more by direct instruction or observation?

- *What does it take to build a strong, positive family that stays connected?*

  We deal with work environments because we want to get paid—effort is expended by everyone in a spirit of collaboration. I was curious as to whether these same concepts apply to a family.

- *What do you believe destroys the unity of a family?*

  Cultural beliefs and defragmentation of a universal value system makes it harder to define what a family actually "is" today. I sought to reveal what other women have experienced and then try to ascertain any destructive trends.

- *What is the hardest decision you ever had to make?*

Until we have an understanding of the inner battle that is waged on issues of significance by a person, we can't judge the choices they made. In the responses to this question, I discovered women face many similar issues.

- *What is the one thing you would do differently in your life?*

Do you believe a life filled with regret colors the future in a negative light? Curious about the path untraveled, I wondered if we're truly defined by our choices and are powerless to change direction.

- *What are the top challenges you face in your work or career?*

The primary basis for this question involved looking for commonalities of experience in the work environment. Are the issues our generation of women faced in carving out a career changing for our daughters?

- *What does it take to build a strong, positive work environment?*

This question focuses on the issues related to creating a managerial process where employees thrive. Perhaps these responses will be the key to more effective recruiting and retention efforts.

- *What do you believe destroys the culture of a business?*

Can we examine impartially our culpability in contributing to a negative company or department culture? But I also wanted to know whether it would be easier for the respondents to identify negative behaviors over recognizing and rewarding positive actions.

- *What do you rejoice in the most?*

I really wanted to know what other women enjoyed and whether those times of joy would it be relationship focused or success oriented.

- *What do you wish to have happen for your children?*

I'm curious in how the generations have changed in terms of building futures for their offspring. Did we give our children the life tools to make the right decisions or have our actions influenced them in ways we didn't expect?

- *What are the top three life lessons women would benefit from knowing?*

Straightforward advice without any strings attached, this seemed like the perfect way to end the journey of self-reflection.

As you read, you'll find out that I don't give you a response to every question. I picked the answers that were the most frequent, or made me think, or laugh, or cry (my editor wanted me to warn you—better get out your tissues for some of these.) I added comments to either highlight the lesson of the response or to comment on the provocative statements just because I had to. You can find the summarized answers to each question in the Appendix at the back of the book; the answers I picked really come from my need to find a way to navigate my own change in life.

And that's what I would like to give you—something to take away and use as you gear up for your second wind. My wish for you is that, by sharing our collective wisdom, we hit our stride and build a purposeful life with grace, fortitude, and tenacity.

But there's something else. Embracing concepts that keep us young at heart and provide a different perspective is just the beginning of the information offered. Maybe, just maybe, we don't have to fight so hard at our age. Our world has evolved, parameters have changed, the old stereotypes don't exist anymore, but perhaps as a generation we don't recognize it yet.

Join me in exploring the hopes, fears, dreams for the future and personal beliefs of 168 women. Perhaps through their eyes you can better understand your own journey. I know I did.

The advice sometimes surprised me, sometimes comforted me. Through their responses, I hope we can all gain insight into our own motives. I want to pass on all the sound advice and options for moving forward these women gave me, but above all, I want you to get what I got most of all—to embrace the future for all the wonder it holds, rather than dreading this next stage in our lives.

We are responsible for the direction our lives take and the attitude with which we address obstacles that may block our path. Essentially, what I've found to be stunningly true is that being women, we share not just a biological reality, but common experiences of frustration, stress, confusion, joy and profound love.

I urge you to identify the responses that resonate with you and answer the questions I've posed with the goal of decreasing isolation and enhancing our conversation. If we take the time to tap into our collective experiences, wisdom ensues.

Survey Details

You may be curious as to where you fit in the demographics of the women who completed the survey. Here is the basic information supplied by the respondents for your reference as you consider the advice that you are about to read.

168   Total Respondents

Marriage Status

18%	Divorced	72%	Married
8%	Never Married	2%	Widowed

Family Size

79%	Had Children	23%	One child
54%	Two children	16%	Three children
4%	Four children	2%	Five children
3%	Six children	1%	Eight children
21%	No children		

Employment

95%   Full time work
    25%   Manager
    36%   Sales (88% Real Estate / 12% Other)
    3%   Professional Services—Attorney, Accountant
    12%   Education (Coaching / Training / Speaker)
    24%   Other
58%   Self-employed
31%   Have second jobs or sources of income
4%   Unemployed

Chapter One

Stronger Than We Know

One of the most consistent words I have found that describes us as a gender, the way we live and face the future, is strength. But why is it we seem to fight against its obvious manifestations? For example, accepting a compliment is one of the hardest lessons I've ever had to learn. A few years back, my best friend commented favorably on my outfit. I immediately informed her of the bargain pricing I got on the pantsuit (my way of seeking validation in the choice I'd made). She touched my arm, smiled kindly and said, "Just say thank you."

It's that simple—just accept the compliment as it is offered. Acknowledging strengths is like that. I've seen employees become flustered when I notice their abilities, yet by the light in their eyes, I know they were delighted about receiving the recognition.

At one point in my management career, my time spent with employees became limited. To encourage ongoing positive reinforcement, I devised a plan. Laminating a photocopy of my right hand, I posted the sheet at shoulder height, hanging a clipboard underneath. I taped a sign next to the photocopy which read, "For a free pat on the back, lean here. Write down what you did well, sign, and date it."

We went through five laminated sheets within six months due to continual use by my direct reports. Each day, I checked the clipboard and located the person who wrote down their success story in order to speak to them about it. I noticed other people started writing down what their peers had done well or read what was on the clipboard and make a purposeful trip to that person's cubicle to congratulate them on a job well done. Positive reinforcement seems like a small thing to do, but like the waves from a pebble dropped into a lake, it spreads outward to a broader reach. Energy can be infectious.

Why don't we acknowledge our strength and accept it boldly and embrace the opportunities that working to our strengths can bring us? Circumstances and upbringing provide the answer to that question. My parents expected me to excel in my education and in sports. However, when I won a scholarship for writing an essay which I slaved over for three weeks, the first thing my mother asked was "Who wrote this?"

What? It's like a child presenting their first drawing of a dog and the parent looks at it, says "That's nice" and then tosses it away. The lesson learned is "do the work, but it really doesn't mean anything to anyone." With enough of those experiences, it is possible that the child starts wondering why they even bother. As women, we often aren't recognized for the work we do or for how effectively we juggle our lives and careers, because, quite frankly, it is just expected of us.

Talking about our strengths could also be perceived as bragging—no one likes a braggart. Or if we do stand out because of an exceptional effort on our part, we sometimes have to run the gauntlet of peer rejection due to jealousy. Bottom line, who needs this anxiety? It's very possible that we start holding back and doing just enough to keep our jobs or maintain our role as a mother, sister, or friend.

Only you can analyze how you embrace your strengths and adapt to the environment in which you live and work. The question is powerful and once you acknowledge your abilities, it's amazing how liberating that can be when you embrace the fact that you matter and you are alright with that!

■ What is your greatest personal strength?

Because we're so weirdly loath to own them, in the survey, I wanted women to identify their strengths. Perhaps because it was in the relative safety of a survey, they did, and I've shared the top five traits from the list. As you read through them, imagine how our relationships with other women could blossom if we took advantage of opportunities to share these characteristics with each other and draw strength from them. Here are the answers to the question: what is your greatest personal strength?

- *Empathetic, care about people, emotional intelligence*
- *Dedication, determination, tenacity, perseverance, and commitment*
- *Positive personality, optimistic point of view*
- *Independent of thought, stand up for what I believe in, visionary*
- *Adaptable, get along with people, understand different points of view*

Notice what was most frequently mentioned; no "hard skills" appeared in the top five strengths such as typing, cleaning, cooking, etc. The responses zeroed in on communication, relationships, outlook on life, and personal independence.

These are elements that commonly appear when discussing leadership traits.

Women are natural born leaders, and we should build more opportunities to have our voices heard and our innate abilities used to the fullest. Let's vow that we'll concentrate on enhancing the strengths we already possess rather than spending untold hours on trying to fix perceived deficiencies. Haven't we spent enough time trying to live up to ideals espoused by others? Benchmarks are needed to stretch professionally and to measure our improvement; but I've learned that identifying the strong aspects of our personalities and abilities is the shortest road to personal satisfaction.

We know what works for us and what doesn't.

Isn't that the key element we embedded into our children— recognizing personal worth and learning to compete internally rather than against the masses? In the book Don Quixote, a dying man envisioned himself straddling a great horse, wearing shiny armor and saving damsels in distress. His complete belief in his vision of reality created such a powerful aura of strength around him, others couldn't help but participate, even if it was for only a short while.

If we are the architect of our own positive reinforcement, we create a happier mindset. If we can move from analyzing our deficiencies to recognizing and utilizing our strengths we can:

- Even out the emotional high and lows

- Establish a consist temperament and life purpose that will allow others to more easily relate to us

- Obtain professional satisfaction and success—especially if we rise to the level of mastery in a particular strength or skill

- Wake up each morning excited and welcoming the day's prospects

I've observed that looking at the "downside" is a common trait shared by women, and I recommend that we evaluate criticisms we receive and determine whether it applies to our situation. If it isn't accurate or relevant, ignore it and move on. Let's put things in perspective and take this opportunity to build our strengths by reframing negative feedback:

The comment:	*It's just like a woman to become emotional about a problem!*
Reframed:	*My ability to empathize with others and relate personally with clients is a powerful reason why I'm trusted in the advice I give.*
The comment:	*You have worked well in an administrative capacity, but we don't see a future for you in management.*
Reframed:	*My expertise at workflow and clear understanding of the daily processes of the various positions makes me a perfect candidate for the management position.*

Take to heart what is relevant to your life experience and emotionally look at criticism with a critical eye in order to move forward in a positive manner. You are stronger than you know. And if we truly embrace our personal strength, we can look realistically at the fears women face each day. Perhaps the next chapter will put your worries in perspective.

Chapter Two

Fear and the Unknown Path

Have you ever had a panic moment when you spied a large insect crawling on a wall next to your shoulder? I have. Heaven forbid if one lands on me during a stroll through a park. The resulting spastic dance compels others to jump to the rescue, convinced I need immediate medical attention. Don't expect to visit a botanical garden with me during daylight hours…I wait until dusk so the bees are exhausted from flitting about all day and have retired for the evening. I've developed an entire system of handling that fear over the years.

Ridiculous? Absolutely.

Some people are averse to heights because looking over a balcony more than three stories from the ground makes their knees turn into jelly. I've sat next to individuals who rock in their seats with their hands clenched together, praying for their safety during a flight because they are convinced the plane will crash. No rational aspect to that at all.

I've become fatalistic in my approach to life—what will be will be. Why waste precious living hours worried about things that are out of my control?

Someone recently asked me how I felt about nuclear proliferation. The immensity of that question is something I simply can't grasp, because once those bombs drop, I know I'll be a survivor. My biggest concern will be what to do if I break or lose my glasses? Forget about radiation poisoning, if I can't see clearly, I'm toast.

The element of fear fascinates me. It took years for me to recognize that my internal war regarding all the fears I harbored was exactly that—my internal war. Others seemed to live their lives just fine in a world that constantly changed the rules. So, the first step in my journey of discovery was to identify and qualify the fears I held and figure out the rationalizations I created in order to keep those fears close to me—thus the questions: What scares you the most? What is your greatest personal fear?

■ What scares you the most? What is your greatest personal fear?

Interestingly enough, the participants to this survey took a broader view of life and named some truly scary issues. Do these fears rule their lives like my bug aversion? It's important for us to realize that fears can create havoc simply by inhibiting our ability to move forward. If we start focusing on all the bad things in life, how can we enjoy what we have in the here-and-now? Personally, I'm amazed at the sheer number of things to be afraid of. So, I'm just going to comment on a few responses, and then I'm locking the door…

- *Losing those you love.*

  Fear of personal death did not appear nearly as frequently as the concern about losing someone we love. Perhaps our lives are validated and documented in memories by those who know us best. To lose that mirror will deprive us of a reflection of our soul.

- *Being alone, unloved, rejected and unappreciated.*

  Does this mean fear of being alone at night with no one to talk to or is it because we fear not having something to occupy our minds and hearts? Humans, by nature, are social animals. But, notice how easy it is for us to cut ourselves off from humanity by filling up each hour with tasks to complete rather than concentrating on being fully present when we are with others. Should we be surprised that we sow what we reap?

If we are filling our time with moments that count, are we ever really destined to be alone? If we continue to exercise our brain and learn to embrace new concepts and ideas, will not our own store of energy carry us through the times of isolation? These are tough questions that only we can answer for ourselves.

- *Getting old and not being able to take care of myself or not being financially secure.*

As we age, time takes on a different significance. We experience the fragility of a deteriorating body and worry about our slowing mental agility. We sigh when our children gather together and forget we are in the room. When will the shift occur when we become a "duty" rather than a destination of choice? Women live longer than males, and as a result, we know we have to make sure our finances last so that we don't move from being a "duty" to a burden on our children. With costs rising each year and incurring debt threatening our ability to stay afloat, this fear is well founded.

I just bought lottery tickets—I'm hedging my bets; someone has to eventually win the pot!

- *Our children thinking that it is normal to have sex immediately after they meet someone.*

With the proliferation of explicit sexual scenes on television and in the movies, our children have celebrity role models flaunting sexuality. I feared our son would pass this adult rite way too soon so I laid down one rule when he was thirteen years old, "When you are thinking you might want to get seriously physical with a young woman, call me first."

Of course, a blank look crossed his face, but he nodded in agreement to the stipulation.

At the age of sixteen, he invited a young girl over to the house and they departed to the lower level. After thirty minutes of unusual quiet, I called his cell phone and when he answered, I asked, "Is it time to call me yet?" He barked out a laugh and chuckled, "No, Mom." The blushing young lady scurried upstairs five minutes later with my son close behind. Mission accomplished.

A few years later, I asked my son why he had never called me when he had his first "moment." He stuttered, "What was I supposed to do? Stop everything and talk to you?" As if it was an unreasonable request.

As an adult, my son realizes the promise to call me was my way of giving him a "caution" light as he considered his actions and the consequences for the young women that could evolve from the sexual act. I gained time to share with him that women treat sex differently, how babies are born, the responsibilities of a father, and that when a woman conjoins with a man, it is a profound moment. Ultimately, I wanted to embed the message that he should respect the woman who shares with him the most intimate of gifts and to handle that relationship with the greatest care.

- *Lack of purpose and moral values in the younger generation as well as their need for instant gratification that borders on a sense of entitlement.*

Let's take a trip back to our younger years; we burned bras, aggressively challenged authority, initiated the evolution of Human Resource management and conceptualized the Internet. Our parents berated us for our long hair and expressions of peace and love.

When we became parents, we gave our children freedom to be themselves and just look at what they did with that independence! Our kids recognized the power of connection by dating in groups, then used advanced technology in order to connect worldwide in a way we never thought possible. As for the lack of ethics, the Baby Boomer generation was accused of not having moral values—remember Woodstock? In reality we stood proudly on our ethics and didn't give in to the status quo without a fight.

- *With that heritage, why would we expect any less from our children and their children?*

I wonder if we need to question why we fear for the moral values of our children. When I ask audiences to raise their hand if they think their personal moral values are very good to excellent, typically 90 percent of the members raise their hands. If that is the case, why do we assume our children weren't listening to us or observing our decision-making processes? Because the social relationship methods are changing, concentrating on what is invaluable in building positive relationships is more productive than fearing the inevitable change.

Personally, I'm astounded by the honesty of the responses in revealing the personal challenges they have endured, and then, how often the same answers were repeated as a fear. The response below, above all the others I received to the question about fear, revealed to me the connection the feminine gender shares. No matter how tough we think we are, the daily burden and emotional aspects of our lives continue to be a driving force behind our fears.

- *And then, if you thought you had it bad… I have a fear that my life won't get any better than this. This year is hard because I just lost a seven-month old grandson, my office flooded with five feet of really awful water, I'm trying to help my elderly mother and mother-in-law, my son's life is currently in chaos and I have two sisters whose health won't let them live much longer.*

There are women who have had their share of surprises and overwhelming circumstances which threaten to defeat them, but consider how strong they've become facing adversity. Someone once told me that God only places as much burden on our shoulders as we can handle.

I can only handle about a half-pound worth of trouble.

Because confusion, stress, and terror just don't do it for me, I evaluate what adventures I'll participate in based upon the worst-case scenario rule. If the worst thing that can go wrong is more than I can endure, I won't participate. Caution, common sense, and foresight all factor into utilizing the worst case scenario evaluation process. Let me demonstrate how this concept works as I share how I made a vacation decision:

In much need of a peaceful, relaxing vacation, my husband, Rick, suggested we take a cruise ship and sail around the Bahamas for a week. We would enjoy the sunlight, bountiful food, entertainment, and beautiful scenery. Sounds perfect, right? Not if you evaluate it carefully for what could go wrong.

I could gain weight.

I'm already struggling with several extra pounds as it is. To be faced with heaps of sumptuous food that you only see in magazines would be too much. I know I would shove my way through the line of other vacationers like a quarterback determined to make a touchdown. Knocking people off their feet would ensue, injuries would be incurred, and my husband's general embarrassment as he helplessly watches would last a lifetime.

No one stands between me, my flaky croissant, and the heavenly chocolate fountain with dipping pretzels and strawberries. No one.

The crew vanishes and there is no one to calm the passengers.

What if the ship experiences physical distress due to a collision with a whale or an iceberg? Friends assure me that the cruise line crew will make heroic efforts to ensure I was safely escorted to a life boat. Sure...remember the ship that sank in North Atlantic? The crew was off the boat before the first leak sprang forth! I've seen the movie *Titanic!* Only the rich and beautiful get on the life raft. I'd be with the rest of the vacationers, overweight, frazzled, and frugal, bobbing in the heaving salt water. Disorientation would set in and I would swim out to sea farther rather than toward land—never to be seen again. My family would have to wait seven years to collect on my life insurance proceeds.

The boat could flip over and sink.

It's possible that a sudden storm could come up and the waves would cause the boat to literally turn over up-side-down. It can happen. I watched the *Poseidon Adventure*—twice. A rogue wave surges over the deck railings, forcing the boat to tilt until it's upside down in the water. Only small pockets of air exist in the entire structure. Besides suffocating to death, metal objects and glass would fly through the air, seeking a person who was not diligent in avoiding streaking missiles. I would develop a twitch as result of desperately watching out for hazards—which in turn would cause me to hyperventilate. Then my hands and feet would cramp up from the lack of oxygen, my husband would have to haul me to safety by lifting me onto his shoulder. He'd take about ten steps and have to place me back down on the ship's ceiling (remember, we're upside down here…) His look of dismay that I'm not the same weight as when we married would pass over his face and he'd consider leaving me behind.

Life boat survivor.

Let's say the crew did remain behind and I did manage to get to safety in a life boat. All on board would expire from dehydration. Since I don't drink liquids often, I would be the lone survivor. First, I'd have to decide what to do with the people who have passed on. Do I keep them in the boat so that their loved ones can bury them properly, or shove them over the side? I could never eat them; someday, a person would ask me "So, Karel, what did you eat to survive when you were out there for so long on that life raft?"

I'd have to answer "Ernie." Not good.

So, I decide to pitch them over the side. Great… a shark feeding frenzy ensues. I'd survive, only to be terrorized by great white sharks and orca whales who mistake my life boat as a seal meal. Hopefully the craft is made of steel and their teeth can't puncture the boat. If it's a rubber boat…I shudder to think about what could happen.

Spending two weeks floating endlessly until I managed to drift into a shipping lane and be rescued is the most likely scenario. However, I'd have to be placed in a mental institution because every time I saw someone's artificially whitened teeth I'd scream, "Shark!"

Drift to an uninhabited land mass.

With my luck, I'd land the boat on the sand beach of an undiscovered, uninhabited island in the middle of nowhere with no one to talk to. That hurts a bit, but I think I could handle it. There would be fruit to eat, but it won't agree with my digestive system and thus give me gas. Monkeys, shrieking from the trees, would pelt me with coconuts. Growling noises in the brush erupt from wild beasts that have eaten the fruit and are having a rougher time with it than I. They aren't happy and want to take their anger out on someone…and then they spot the suburban wife. I'd have to fight them off with my purse.

A side note here…my purse goes with me everywhere. You never know when you will need your smart phone, pen, lipstick and credit card.

Successful in fending off the wild animals, I'd realize I was starving slowly to death. Dehydration isn't an issue because I've landed on a tropical island and it rains continually throughout the day. All I have to do is lie on my back with my mouth open and the torrential downpour will provide me with enough fresh water to survive.

Food is what I need. What are my choices? I don't know how to cook and haven't a clue as to how to start a fire without a Coleman stove, charcoal, or lighting devices. The only choice will be to eat fish, bugs and worms—raw. I've watched the television show, Fear Factor. Devour live bugs and raw flesh, are you kidding? The live bug I happen to swallow whole would be a tenacious survivor and eventually find its way out of my body. Do I want to be there when it discovers the way out? No way!

So wait, I'm down to eating grass, leaves, and bark. A rather colorful meal—Granola and salad. Now, I can live with that. I'd lose weight, become suntanned, and my hair would gain lovely highlights. My singing would be perfected as no one would tell me to stop yodeling, and my agility skills would improve as I dodged coconut shells.

In reality, by identifying our fears, we can address them. Ask yourself what you fear and determine the level of adjustment that you are making in your life to accommodate that fear. My challenge to you is to stop calculating the worst case scenario and shift to evaluating what you can gain. If your "worse case" is absurd—acknowledge that and then show up. We have fears, but there are ways to handle it by talking to others, learning more about what is behind the fear and gaining a perspective that will help you to release the anxiety and move forward. If you do this for yourself on a consistent basis, you'll be amazed at the possibilities that will enter your life.

Once we move from the intimate sphere of our own experiences, our observations of what is going on around us take on a new light. In the next chapter, discover how the perspectives of these women carry over into their world view.

Chapter Three

A Sound Bite World

Perhaps I've not been as observant of our world as I should be. Last January, I subscribed to nine different business magazines and began to read them as soon as they arrived. Diligently educating myself on foreign affairs, trying to figure out who ran what in our government and how to invest my meager funds effectively, I started to feel overwhelmed.

This passionate immersion lasted two months.

When I began avoiding the mailbox, my husband brought in the magazines and started to stack them alongside my desk. Perhaps it would have been wiser to only order two magazines and start there, but I really wanted to have a broad perspective of what others had written about current events.

Instead of feeling satisfied about my newly gained perspective, a cloud of negativity hovered over my head. I became restless at night and began dreaming of lost income, abandoned opportunities, violent home invasions, and of governments that supported entitlement attitudes. Often, I would surge awake fuming or sobbing in gulps of air.

My husband became puzzled by the loss of my positive attitude. No matter what happened in the world, Rick could empathize with victims, shake his head in disgust at a new political endeavor, and still at the end of the day appreciate the joys around him. I decided I could use him as my buffer. I prioritized what I actually wanted to know about the world and assigned the responsibility of informing me about these issues to my stalwart man. He manages this role faithfully and completely. I now focus proactively on world realities that I can actually handle. I trust Rick and his no-spin zone as well as his steel-trap memory; nothing like having a card catalog for a husband who also can relate to events with a historical perspective.

If you're not emotionally equipped to handle the rampant negative news that crashes on us daily, I urge you to acknowledge it. Only by recognizing what we can't handle, can we enter into a frame of mind that is conducive to creating a solution in how to filter that information. Some people tune into a single talk radio program or others only watch the morning news and then have the entire day to absorb, reflect, and react. The primary objective is to keep apprised of critical information, but receive the news in a manner that best fits your ability to cope. You can learn from the responses to the question below: How do you feel about the world we live in today using a few defining words?

■ How do you feel about the world we live in today using a few defining words?

It's about balancing rational fear with relevant information as well as maintaining an attitude of personal accountability to define our own world perspective. It is evident that perceptions of our current cultural situation have created an environment of personal and professional fear. Quite frankly, the report card from these women is much more negative than I expected.

I wonder if I'm residing on the same planet. Perception is reality.

- *Fast paced, busy*
- *Exciting, hopeful, optimistic, incredible potential*

- *Information driven, intelligent, divisive*
- *Chaos, changing, evolving, unsettled, unlimited consequences, lack of balance, unpredictable*
- *Too technology-focused, over-connected, information overload*

Notice how the top responses relate to the speed and manner in which the world evolves with or without our help. A social revolution is in full force, redefining the way we communicate and interact with each other. The future is no longer something that "is coming." The technology wave is here and like a tsunami, it will overwhelm anything in its path. And the younger generation is the catalyst for this change, rushing forward to gain their piece of the next new thing. As a Baby Boomer, I realize that I no longer have the luxury of wishing things would just slow down. For people in my age bracket, there is a sense of helplessness in being able to harness the energy that is catapulting us into a new reality. It's change coming at us and delivered through a fire hose.

Interestingly enough, the novel *1984* by George Orwell (copyrighted in 1949) already identified much of what we are experiencing now. If he could visualize the massive technology and cultural changes then, why couldn't we do so and prepare for it mentally? I believe that sometimes when things feel so different, we have a tendency to hide our heads and hope it will pass.

That's what I did until I realized the way people relate now in our world is more far-reaching and much more intimate in sharing experiences than I ever imagined. Bottom line, if I didn't somehow find a way to understand and use new technology, I very well may not be able to relate to or communicate with my child and future grandchildren. This concern alone compelled me to learn more about the technology that makes sense to me and embrace it.

So, after reading these responses, I took a trip on Twitter. com—a virtual exploration for the purpose of learning as much as possible about this communication venue. The process of sending an update to people who chose to follow your "streaming thoughts" is called tweeting. The first thing I thought when I heard the term Twitter it was what people did on the long train ride as shown in a scene from *The Music Man* written by Meredith Willson: "talk a lot, talk a lot, cheep, cheep, cheep." The passengers exchange information and gossip at an astounding rate as they barrel forward to their destination.

Jumping onto the train of sharing information, our on-line social networking is about small bits of information being tossed out to the virtual world, and if you're lucky, someone grabs onto the sound bite and decides to follow your comments. It is Internet blogging in shorthand.

Reading a few of the tweets made me feel my age. It truly is a brave new world out there and as a solidly placed Baby Boomer, I'm trying to adapt with as little personal anxiety as possible. The first hurdle to get over…why would anyone care what I am doing at a particular moment? My husband only checks in on me once a day, much less several times in a ten hour period. And in that single conversation with Rick, we cover all of the interesting and bland things that occurred during the day. While enjoying a hot meal, glasses are clinked, jokes are exchanged and personal observations are enjoyed; total time—thirty minutes. How do I write about that in 140 characters?

The art of communication encourages digging deeply for the resonance of the relationship, not skittering across the surface like a water bug. How can we best represent our thoughts on such a venue as Twitter without having the opportunity to develop a concept to its fullest? That is the challenge we face in acknowledging the rapid changes associated with technology. According to E. H. Schein, the most important thing for people to understand is what goes on inside their own heads. Improvements in technology provide a venue to do just that—corresponding on a social network in a non-threatening environment. Experiencing a world in constant change can feel like chaos and it causes us to be emotionally unsettled. Let's face it; we have been raised with advice that consists of the following:

- Steady as she goes
- Slow and steady wins the race
- Look before you leap

Each statement stresses the need to slow down first before making any change…to be methodical in our decision making process. However, the world isn't going to wait for us anymore. Our children, reared on computers, debit cards, and iPods®, are mentally prepared to leap quickly and embrace change as a natural form of life.

If our world is too busy, face paced, and scary…well, all that means is that we're not processing all of the information fast enough. Perhaps our biggest concern is that we know misperception can occur if we move too quickly, then we "allow" ourselves to respond emotionally to our interpretation without being aware that it is based on incorrect information. Ultimately, connecting in a sound bite world means we probably need to make a greater effort to ensure our relationships are based on clear communication. The steps to accomplish this involve the following:

- First, let's make sure our perceptions of a situation, conversation, or written material are accurate. That means validating the information before deciding the action you wish to take.

- Paraphrase back what an individual tells you so that you can be sure what you heard is accurate, or by asking follow-up, open-ended questions until you receive all of the facts. It may take a bit more time, but you'll dramatically increase the reliability and accuracy of the communication exchange.

- React appropriately. Better yet, wait to react until you have all the information in hand. Our initial response may be an emotional one. Learn to hold that in check until you really know whether you have something to react to emotionally or not!

- Believe that there will be a positive resolution to any communication issue. A forward looking outlook can help smooth interpersonal relationships. There isn't anything that can't be fixed unless the other party doesn't cooperate.

- Finally, learn to deal with people problems directly. It is often the behavior of the individual that causes the uproar. Address those behaviors directly and you are well on your way to smoothing out the communication process and establishing a better likelihood of a positive resolution.

Technology has changed the ground rules of building relationships. Our younger generation has not lost the ability to chat or hold a conversation. They just do it with their thumbs on a smart device—sound bites of information delivered at lightning speed. I've begun texting my son and quite frankly, I feel closer to him because I know he is on his phone as we text. I realize

I can call him, but there is something exciting about waiting for the "you've got mail" ping on my phone.

By acknowledging how my life is better through the enhancements that are occurring everyday on objects, I have stepped up to being more responsible for my personal filtering system. I may be texting now, but that doesn't mean I have to check out every single "ap" that is available for my iPhone. I chose to concentrate on finding the technology that helps me meet my personal objectives. So, to get closer to my son and accommodate my clumsy fingers, I purchased the smart phone and learned how to use it.

However, some people live in a state of being that encourages chaos. If that isn't right for you, then get proactive by:

1. Creating the communication boundaries you can live with. For example, I never answer the phone during a meeting with clients. Personally, I feel its vital people know I'm fully concentrating on them during that time and not distracted by addressing the next call.

2. World change and technology advances are only going to speed up. Determine for yourself which technology works for you and dive in with both feet. I purchased an iPhone two years ago and now I can't remember what it was like just to have a "regular" phone. Having photos, music and Scrabble at my fingertips is just plain thrilling!

3. If you feel like you have a lack of balance and unable to find your footing in this sea of change, don't worry. The person next to you is probably feeling the same thing. Technology is like hooking a monster fish and feeling the stress of trying to reel it into the boat. Once you

"let go" and the line goes slack, initially you stumble and experience a feeling of loss. However, the sense of unbalance quickly passes. There is always the next big fish. Technology is like that—it gets more user-friendly as it evolves. So passing up on one version today and waiting for the enhancement might just be a smart thing to do.

4. To keep things simple, identify exactly what you want in terms of technology for your life. Once you know the "what," you can go in search of someone who knows the "how" and "where." The more specific you are in your needs, the easier it is to identify the type of technology you should purchase or change you should make. Otherwise, life will continue to be chaotic and you will constantly be asking "what happened?"

Twitter and other networks will shift and evolve and you don't want to be left behind. Reach out and touch someone. And to show you how easy it is, here is a 138-character Tweet that sums up this entire chapter:

> *Twitter set us free to exchange ideas, concepts and recommendations in a quick and effective manner. Sound bites to connect with purpose.*

Impressions from Mother

When I was seventeen, going on my first formal date, my mother announced as I left the house, "Never be a service station for any man." I just about stumbled down the front steps when I heard that. Closely followed with a mumbled, "Men don't buy the cow when they can get the milk for free!" she shut the door behind me.

Yup, that's my mom's version of telling me chastity is a virtue and tying it into the economic system. I had visions of drive-through gas stations that served up sex rather than gas. Being warned not to give up something I really didn't know about confused me. Did that mean no holding hands or kissing? When would I actually know that I had entered into the service zone?

Even though she never cleared *that* one up for me, she did give me a lot of great advice. In fact, lessons we learned from our mothers were astutely practical. For example:

- *"Do it right the first time!"*

  Remember how a "halfway" job would not pass your mother's inspection? She wouldn't correct our error—we had to. We learned quickly that by doing it right the first time, it saved us time in the long run.

- *"Make sure you can always take care of yourself financially— rely upon no one, not even your husband."*

  Whatever happened to Prince Charming? Wasn't our knight in shining armor supposed to ride up on an elegant steed, sweep us off our feet, and plant us in a majestic castle where every wish we had would be fulfilled? Isn't that how the story is supposed to go? What's this? We're supposed to take care of ourselves? Ridiculous.

Funny thing however, the more we took advantage of career openings and the more we learned the better opportunities came our way. Raising our hand, relishing a chance to explore our capabilities rather than fearing failure, we created a career resume which ultimately enhanced our family's financial well-being. Granted, not all of our ventures have been successful, but with each we've gained another experience, ready to utilize the wisdom gleaned in a future endeavor.

Was I the only one that received odd yet applicable advice? Truly wanting to know what other mothers taught their daughters, I asked the question: What lessons did you learn from your mother?

■ What lessons did you learn from your mother?

The responses from the 168 women varied dramatically on the advice their mothers gave them from funny to poignant to downright hilarious.

- *No job is beneath you—don't let circumstances dictate who you are.*

  Dignity is a precious element to our self-esteem. Many of us have had to face doing menial jobs in order earn money to buy food or clothe our children. Our work does not define who we are; it's an extension of our circumstances. We do what is necessary. That is one of the reasons my best friend, Carol, fully acknowledges waiters who serve her and clerks who check out her purchases at a retail store. What they do is not who they are. Wise advice.

- *Choose your battles.*

Women know intimately what this statement means. We don't obsess about the jeans our child is going to wear to school, choosing instead to spend our energies in making sure they make intelligent choices in friends and not give in to peer pressure to try street drugs. I'm still waging the battle of the baseball hat. My son insists on wearing the hat inside a public place. He firmly believes humanity should not be subjected to his hat head, and I am adamant that it is a sign of respect to the proprietor to remove his hat.

Stalemate.

- *Take care of yourself; no one else will.*

Women don't lose sight of their companionship need, but we also realize statistically that a day may come when we are alone to face paying the bills. At an early age, my mother created a true entrepreneur, urging me to establish my own long-term career. For the decision-making process, she cautioned me to consider, "What is the worst thing that can happen? And if it does happen, can you afford it?" Whether she was referring to asking for a salary increase or giving relationship advice, it still rings true today.

Decisions relating to my career are instinct-driven and her method of analyzing risk helps me create specific strategic plans. Financial and personal independence is becoming even more important to women today considering the high divorce rate. It never hurts to plan ahead.

- *Never forget you were a couple first; you need to work at any kind of relationship to maintain it and have them flourish.*

"Once the kids were grown and out of the house, we didn't seem to have anything in common anymore." I've heard those horror tales of men leaving their wives for women half their age—the term I believe is "trophy wife." People fall in and out of love for a variety of reasons. We want to be able to blame someone, but unless we know all of the intimate details of the relationship, how can we begin to assign blame? All we can do is make every effort to be fully present for those we love and try to create opportunities to have shared experiences.

When our son, Ben, was five years old, I traveled nationally for up to two weeks at a time. After an uncharacteristically long trip, I arrived home to the arms of my loving husband. Passion flared quickly, but was interrupted by the excited chattering of our son, brandishing a stick of some sort he had just found. We gave him the attention he needed, and then returned to our affectionate embrace.

Ben shoved between us and started another babbling dialog. We could see that our moment might have trouble advancing to the next stage unless we could distract this child. I called our neighbor, Sue and asked her to look out for Ben who would be running outside any minute. She welcomed me home and agreed to devote thirty minutes for child care.

I retreated to the kitchen and pulled out the Oreo Cookie bag and asked Ben if he wanted some. His eyes opened wide at the unexpected treat, reaching up for the sack. I quickly wrapped several cookies in aluminum foil and I headed to the back door with Ben close on my heels jumping for the snack the whole way.

Flinging open the door, I spotted Sue, nodded my head and heaved the cookies as far as I could into the back yard. Ben shot out the door, crossed the deck and slid across the grass until he clutched the cookies. My neighbor laughed so hard it echoed though the neighborhood.

Quality time, nothing like it.

- *Tomboys are not popular at prom time.*

Most young girls can't wait to wear the evening gown for the ultimate date, the high school prom. There's something about dressing up like an adult woman that sends a tingle down our spine. This rite of passage for me never happened and even as I sit here today, I feel a pang of regret. Maybe if I had worn skirts more often or stopped showing off my bicep muscles, a boy might have asked me to a prom.

Wikipedia indicates that the word tomboy has been around since 1553, used primarily to describe a "rude, boisterous boy." Historically, tomboys have been defined by "boyish" behavior (like more physically active, technological, and scientific interests) and wearing boys' clothing. Another distinction is a tomboy's preference to befriend boys rather than other girls.

And that is where the problem lies…Boys don't date their best friend who knows their deepest fears and secrets.

Today, I realize that my masculine way of thinking and low voice may have been a true asset in my career. But it wasn't until I touched into my feminine intuition and empathy that I truly transformed my management ability. Maybe in our children's children generation the word tomboy may disappear all together…or it will be accepted as a badge of courage rather than a brand of shame to our gender.

- *No one likes a smart ass.*

Typically, women tend to blend in, preferring harmony over dissention. Additionally, people in control don't like it when their authority is challenged. Yet, why do we love to watch verbal sparring matches?

You know a smart ass by the twinkle in their eye when they respond back to a disciplinarian "dressing down," with a sharp witty remark. Usually it stops the other person in their tracks while snickers are heard from the gallery of onlookers. Oh, to have that type of bravery and quick wit.

This next statement actually made me laugh out loud and merits being singled out, not for its wisdom but for its absurdity!

- *Do not stare at people who have disabilities or your children may be born with the same thing.*

The advice goes on and on, but one of the earliest readers of the book, Katie Hesse, a very astute thirty-something, summed it up best:

> *"It feels like the mantra of the old feminist guard. But I find largely that I'm not pushed into these stereotypes of previous generations. In my world as a woman, I struggle with my own need to be an equal contributor rather than society's need to suppress my equality."*

Do you realize the impact of those words? We succeeded in creating an environment for our children to be evaluated based upon their individual contribution rather than limited to expectations associated with gender. Our efforts in reframing our culture and society attitudes have not gone unnoticed or unrewarded.

While my mother wasn't consistent in her words and actions (do as she said, not what she did), her belief that I should benefit by the wisdom she gained as a result of her experiences were paramount to my survival in the world. Somewhere along the line, we listened to our mothers and passed on what we knew to be true: each adventure, insight and relationship, fine-tuning the advice from the previous generation. Like a close band of gypsies sitting around a campfire, we passed on advice and told stories to enhance each other's opportunities.

It's just what families do.

In the next chapter, where I share my mother's story, reflect on the depth of your relationship with your mother and envision how you want that relationship to look. I really wanted to interact with my mother beyond the superficial day-to-day; I wanted to know her.

For those of you who have a difficult or distant connection with your mother, I urge you to find a way to come together adult-to-adult by letting her know the lessons you learned from her and showing her the lessons you can share. It's never too late to make your remaining time together valuable, uplifting, and memorable.

Chapter Five

Reflections of the Past

I wonder if, as an infant, I cried a lot in frustration because I'm an individual who doesn't define myself by how others view me. Being female is the physical aspect of my being, but it isn't what I am in my entirety. I believe the essence of who we are is revealed through our actions and treatment of others. Our spirit shines through our eyes as we gaze upon another human being and share this journey of life.

How, exactly, are women judged: by our gender or as people? The women who responded to the survey had lives shaped by the culture they inhabited and the strength of the role models they learned from. What influences have you experienced in your life?

As promised, I'm going to share my mother's story. As you read, I hope you recognize, as I did, that expectations for women have continued to evolve. For a moment, consider what it must have been like for my mother and her generation…

In 1923, my mother, Dolores, entered the world as the eldest daughter of seven children during the pre-depression era to a family of Polish decent. Hope and despair walked hand in hand. People on Polish Hill were poor, but strong willed and determined to better themselves. Because money was scarce, families grew their own food or bartered for goods, a harsh environment for trying to carve out a living.

Dolores knew what being the oldest female in her Polish-American family meant cooking, cleaning, and taking care of the younger children. Her parents expected her to marry someone before she became an old maid at twenty-five and start the family cycle all over again. Photos of a young Dolores reveal a woman with lush brown hair floating around her aristocratic face, the proud tilt of her head and direct expression showing a woman who understood personal purpose and destiny. But behind that gaze lay a story of frustration and resignation.

As a child, Dolores was often found head bent over a searing hot stove, canning vegetables for the winter. She worked under the watchful eye of her mother scrubbing the kitchen floor, ironing clothes, darning socks, gardening, cleaning the dishes, and sitting with the smaller children. If the chores were not done, a long leather strap hung on the wall and threatened all. Punishment, delivered harshly and quickly, often while she continued with the task, warned there was no room for error.

Death made frequent visits to neighborhood households and took the lives of small children indiscriminately. It seemed survival of the hearty, completion of duties, and loyalty to the family helped ward off Death. Dolores recalled the small white caskets of the babies displayed in the living room of her neighbor's homes, so small, the babies had no chance.

At age fifteen, Dolores's seventh brother, George, was born with a heart condition. He cried incessantly, especially at night while Dolores cradled the infant in her arms. She couldn't rest, afraid she might roll over the baby in her sleep. At the age of six months, George died of a heart attack during the middle of one night while Dolores slept. Dolores looked at the small bundle in her arms when she awoke and understood why she had slept through the night for the first time in weeks. She never recovered from the guilt. Seeing that small pallid face, tiny hands lying peacefully beside the emaciated body, Dolores vowed to find a way to go to school and become a nurse.

Her parents, angry and frustrated with her desire to have a career rather than focus on marriage, refused to assist her in any way. Their denial only made her more determined. The glint of rock hard determination appears in all the photos of Dolores, an almost "I dare you" look.

At age seventeen, Dolores was accepted by Michael Reece Hospital in Chicago as a student. The nursing program pushed students to their physical limit by having them work twelve-hour days, every day, for three years. She suffered through routine hand and nail checks, hairstyle review, and weekly weigh-ins to expel any pregnant students. Dolores endured the polio epidemic of Chicago with over 350 pediatric patients in enforced isolation who fought debilitating fevers, paralysis, and respiratory attacks which eventually resulted in use of the Iron Lung.

The final session of training occurred in the psychiatric ward of the hospital. That's when Dolores learned about the true nature of mental illness. Eighty women started in the Michael Reece nursing program, but only thirty graduated; Dolores, one of them.

She joined the Army's last group of nurses recruited in Chicago and sailed on a Red Cross ship to Manila Bay in the Philippines. Devastation greeted her—hulls of bombed ships projected out of the azure colored water and warnings of Japanese occupation in the hills broadcast over the loud speakers. The lush greenery, so far removed from Chicago, made her catch her breath, startled at the beauty that surrounded her. Purpose, pride, determination, and talent merged as she used her skills to save the ravaged bodies of young soldiers.

Dolores married my father in Manila on Christmas Day and returned to the United States where she eventually reunited with him. Their family expanded by five children that included two sets of twins eighteen months apart. With no other option, Dolores continued to work, first in a doctor's office, as a private duty nurse, then running a nursing home, and finally becoming an instructor of a Licensed Practical Nurse program at a local college.

At the age of 80, her name was engraved on the plaque of the World War II nurses monument in Washington, D.C. Her expression of accomplishment and pride at hearing the news still sends shivers down my spine.

My mother made her vision of a nursing career happen through sheer determination and taking advantage of the opportunities as they arose. Her sense of personal power instilled the concept of remarkable persistence in all of her children and gave me the strength to move forward, regardless of what life threw at me.

So, in honor of our mothers and their tenacity and drive, let's commit to the beacon of possibilities by which we live our lives. And if we end up on that rocking chair, gazing out at a verdant lawn with a cup of coffee in our hand, let our thoughts be on cherishing what we have created rather than what we never achieved or lost.

Life is simply too short.

Chapter Six

Father Rules

In a way, it's easy to see the legacy our mothers gave us. Relationships with our fathers, however, are often a bit more complex. But their lessons and legacy are just as important.

The Lincoln Memorial in Washington, D.C. portrays a strong fatherly expression. The confident set of Abraham Lincoln's facial features instills a sense of security in me even as the penetrating look strips me bare no matter where I stand in the monument public space. This statute exemplifies my father's demeanor.

Many women view their fathers as the knight in shining armor, ready to strike down any errant boy who breaks their heart. They usher us down the aisle and hand us over to our future husbands with a hard glinted smile and stern look that warns, "I'm watching you." The groom quakes and we smile.

Dad, our hero and great protector…Sounds like a movie script. And when we build them up and put them on such a high pedestal, it's easy to tumble off. Imagine, these manly men trying to relate to their daughters even when they think women are impossible to figure out. But understanding innately the desire of daughters who want to please their fathers, they invented the greatest technique in a father's child-rearing arsenal—the "don't disappoint me" tool.

At the age of seventeen, I attended a teen party across town from my house. My curfew set for midnight seemed hours away. I had the pleasure of engaging in a great conversation and hand-holding with a handsome young man. He lived in another town, and life just didn't seem fair that the magic of this night wouldn't be repeated for a long while. I checked the clock and squeaked in dismay that midnight loomed. I called home and my father picked up the line…he obviously had been sitting by the phone.

"Dad, I was wondering if I could extend the curfew to 1:00 a.m. I've met this really great guy!"

Silence.

"Dad, are you there?"

"Yes," he replied in a calm tone.

"It's only another hour, is that okay? This boy lives really far away and I won't be able to see him again for awhile! Can I come home at 1:00?" I begged.

"Honey, you know what the curfew is and where I stand. You make up your own mind, and I'll see you when you come home." My father hung up the phone.

The sound of disappointment in my father's voice was too much to handle; I returned home by 11:50 p.m. What mastery he demonstrated by placing the burden on my shoulders to make the decision when he knew all along that I wouldn't pick a boy over disappointing him. That man knew me better than I knew myself.

My father passed away in 1988 and I never really knew what made him tick. He worked in the media (television and radio), loved sports, and was mayor of our hometown. The community statewide mourned his death. I still vividly recall elements of his persona:

- *Black–cherry tobacco wafting from the pipe clenched between his teeth*
- *Fedora felt hat that emphasized his black glasses*
- *Television tuned to sports*

I remember events ever better!

- *Speaking to audiences as a news anchor then as mayor*
- *Clutching his left arm as he walked me down my wedding aisle while he whispered jokes to make me laugh*
- *Golfing on a summer day*

At my father's death bed, we finally connected in a deeply human way by sharing fears and secrets while my husband and son watched from the corner of the room. My father regretted not being emotionally available to me for most of my life but assured me that it would change with his death. This pragmatic person then declared that people who love you come and help you cross over. For him, it was his deceased mother. Dad promised that he would guide me for as long as I remained alive and when my time came to die, he would come for me.

Huh?

I immediately told him he wasn't allowed in the bathroom or our master bedroom and not to leap out of any closets or suddenly appear in mirrors. Dad laughed until his IV threatened to dislodge. From the moment of his death, as promised, I've felt his presence and have learned to trust my intuition which I believe is guided by him.

As you read the responses to this question regarding the lessons we have learned from our fathers, recognize the stark differences in the answers between a mother's advice and a father's perspective. Teaching us to be strong seems to be a common thread:

- *Toughen up and keep your chin up and out.*
- *Don't let the world get to you.*
- *Don't ever let them see you cry.*

Stoic, solid advice from fathers varies greatly from the typically gentle lessons we gained from our mothers. The survey, however, showed evidence of fathers who felt humble pride for helping their daughters find their way in a troubled world and this gave me hope. Fathers, wise to the world, cautioned their daughters, and it became evident that they only wished to make the path to adulthood easier. Their lessons were important to me, so I asked: "What lessons did you learn from your father?"

■ What lessons did you learn from your father?

The strong thread of encouraging personal strength and non-conformity seemed to be consistent across these responses. Get ready for some answers that practically jump off the page due to the force of the emotion.

- *Keep your word—hold true to your commitments and obligations.*

  The first thing I envisioned when I read this piece of advice was a firm handshake between two men sealing a deal. As men grip hands, they look each other in the eyes and measure the worth of the other man while locking in the commitment. Men understand that their word is their bond—the fundamental element of personal accountability.

Typically, men perceive women as having a "changeable" nature, minds that can shift in a blink of the eye. This advice cautions us to remember that if we aren't reliable and can't be counted on, you really are no good to anyone. Remember how hard it was for women to enter into active combat in the military? We, as women, had to prove we could be counted on to "have the other person's back."

Our fathers tried to prepare us to compete in a man's world by exposing us to the concepts of trust and reliability. We may not be able to shake hands man-to-man, but we can address each other eye-to-eye.

- *Anything worth having in life is worth working for.*

Entitlement is a word that turns sour in a hard-working man's mouth; no one likes a slacker. Do any of these phrases ring a bell?

- ¤ Roll up your sleeves.
- ¤ You can take a break when the work is done.
- ¤ Hard work never killed anyone.
- ¤ The world doesn't owe you anything; you have to work for it.

By example, we discovered that to move ahead in the world we have to put our heads down and work long hours. This work ethic is a primary reason many of us didn't see our fathers as much as we may have liked. My grandfather taught me to work the first eight hours of each day for the paycheck then work the next four hours of the day for myself. No wonder I've been self-employed since 1993.

- *Stay out of trouble; everyone reads the police logs. You're never above the consequences.*

Fathers sure know how to lay down the law and impress upon young minds the dire consequences for actions we might do without thinking. They might not always be there to protect us and the best they can do is caution us against stupid acts against people and property. As a result, we gained critical thinking skills by learning the fundamentals of cause and effect. For every action there is a reaction and a possible consequence. That is why I believe women have developed incredible planning capabilities thus earning the title "the family social directors."

- *As long as you eat at my table and live under my roof you will be respectful of me.*

It's difficult standing up for yourself when you're threatened with poverty and the potential of living under a bridge. Initially we may envision a man who loves to strong-arm his family and demand respect even if he has done nothing to earn it. But upon reflection, I believe it goes deeper than that. In a highly competitive corporate environment, men can feel threatened or feel so emasculated at their work, that when they arrive home, the last thing they want to experience is disrespect from their family. If they can't feel like a man in their own house, then where?

Respect from our children is not guaranteed. If we fail to appreciate what our children bring to the table, why should they have any admiration for us? At a minimum, the best we can hope to achieve is our child's deference to our position in the family as the parent. If we earn esteem and respect by valuing the integrity of our children, then a supportive relationship can flourish.

- *If you can't pay cash, you can't afford it.*

Retirees understand that with a fixed income, each purchase needs to be considered carefully before actually buying the object. If something is bought today, what will they have to live without a year from now?

Our fathers came from an era of understanding the value of having cash, knowing that with cash, a person could position themselves to take advantage of future opportunities. Therefore, credit became a dirty word and to be avoided at all costs.

Somewhere along the line, our generation got tired of waiting for the good things and reformatted the message into "credit is good, credit is great." When we were young, our earning capacity appeared endless. Debt really wasn't a problem; we could buy what we wanted when we wanted it and worried about paying for it later. That is until something happened like illness, an accident, or a divorce.

If you daydream about wondering what life would be like if you didn't have debt, that's easy to answer; you'd actually own what you have and have a clear picture of your financial viability.

As I read through the rest of the survey responses, I collated the answers, and placed them into categories; a few elicited an emotional reaction immediately from me, ranging from a smile of recognition to a wince of shared pain. Two of the best were:

- *"Slow down. Always take time for a watermelon break and play because life is too short; fill your life with something positive."*

- *"To not beat your spouse—my father was not a nice man."*

Some of us were lucky and had great dads. But all of us have learned that what our parents are isn't what we have to become. Anger at what never existed should be replaced with what we can create instead. So, if we lack a personal relationship with our father, it might be reasonable for us to strive and make sure we're available to our children, and demonstrate through our relationships how a man respectfully treats a woman and gives love unconditionally. Personally, I believe our actions have to match with our beliefs in order to give our children a fighting chance in this world.

The only way we can erase an unacceptable past is by moving forward and establishing a new way of doing things. I suggest we stop dwelling on what wasn't and focus on what can be. Who knows where it just might lead?

Direct advice is a powerful tool in formulating our life path as well as being aware of the impact of the lessons we learned as we watched our parents interact. The next chapter explores the "hidden" principles our parents may or may not have intended to teach us.

Chapter Seven

Do as I Say...Not as I Do

Parental relationships broadcast important information to children. As a child, you quickly learn what tone of voice conveys respect and caring, and what types of personal contact can border on abusive. "Do as I say, not as I do," rings with a truth that is undeniable. If someone had told me not to steal, but then kept the extra change given to them by mistake, what is the message? What actually constitutes stealing?

Interaction between those we look up to designs the map we might follow as adults. And the messages the women received from their parents proved to range all across the board. How a child perceives a relationship is decoded through a childish viewpoint. What can a five-year-old really understand about how a marriage should work? We might be surprised.

When my son was in his early teens, I asked him, "How does your father show love?" His answer was quick and decisive, "He never misses a game that my team is playing." Curious, I then asked, "What have you learned by watching us?" Shrugging, he responded, "It's a good thing Dad cooks instead of you."

As an adult male, our son treasures his wife, demonstrates boundless love in his hugs, and shows no fear in the kitchen. He observed us and has modeled his behavior accordingly. As parents, we are honored and humbled at the same time to see a reflection of our relationship in the new one he is building.

Unfortunately, some of us learned harsh lessons through watching our parents and have consciously worked to erase the negative impact from our relationships. This determination to have a better life hasn't been an easy path, but I hope we all realized over the years that we can only impact what we can, and we have to leave the rest behind us, acknowledging it is over and done with. What I do know for sure is that we grew a generation that is more self-empowered than we ever dreamed possible.

Below are a few responses from the women regarding how actions spoke louder than words.

■ What did you learn about life by observing your parents?

I don't believe anything is more powerful than the impact of behavior on how we perceive each other. Body language behaviorists teach us that communication consists of 10 percent of the spoken word and the rest is deciphered through body language and action. Therefore, how we perceive love, dedication, teamwork, sacrifice, and working out issues is gleaned through observation. By recognizing the power of our personal childhood imprinting, perhaps we can grow to understand what motivates and guides us as adults.

Read on to discover the profound messages other women learned from observing their parents. Perhaps a few will resonate with you.

- *You don't have to have money to be "wealthy."*

  One of the most famous books ever written, "Christmas Carol," by Charles Dickens centers on the positive impact of Tiny Tim, whose loving spirit made the world a brighter place. The happy memories we evoke usually don't involve something we purchased. Typically we chose to concentrate on the feeling of a moment and the textures that relate to that memory; a calloused hand held tightly in our own, air filled with the smell of burning autumn leaves, or the expression of joy at a compliment.

- *Love can be expressed beyond words.*

How do you express your love without vocalizing it? Is it a glance intended to provide support at a critical moment, a squeeze of the shoulder to let the other person know things will work out okay, or do you pour it in with the ingredients of the bundt cake you're baking? My husband shows love through small gestures; coffee placed at my elbow before I even know I want it, placing a printout of directions on my materials to ensure I don't get lost, or cooking all our meals.

I believe voicing our love is also important. I encourage you to let those you love know frequently the value you place on them being a part of your life. How that takes place is the fun part. I periodically call my son and as soon as he answers, I belt out a song like, "Oh what a beautiful morning..." His laughter is my reward. I wonder if he has warned his wife.

- *Things aren't always what they appear to be.*

Some parents are skilled at hiding conflict from their children, often done to protect them from some unpleasant aspects of life such as money problems, or the fact their parents have grown apart. Children don't have to know everything. Sometimes they're too young to understand what is happening. Parents have to judge which situations should be concealed and what are exposed to daylight.

We can only respond to the information our parents choose to provide. They realize they may be judged on the incomplete data they provide. If our parents choose to keep silent, we have no alternative other than to accept it and move on, hoping that all will be revealed in its own time, if at all.

Hidden information isn't always bad news. Wealth might be downplayed because parents may feel it is important for a child to grow up with an understanding of hard work, dedication toward goal completion, and the satisfaction of a job well done. I once observed an Iowa farmer walking into an auto dealership wearing bib overalls and scraping manure off his shoes. Several experienced salesmen ignored him, but a young woman strode forward and welcomed him to the store. I watched this lady show off the Lincoln Continental vehicles and suppress a flinch when the farmer climbed into the front seat and settled down on the plush white leather.

Within a few minutes, the farmer nodded his head quickly, stood up and said "I'll take it!" Startled by the quick decision, the young woman inquired as to how he wanted to finance the purchase. The grizzled older man handed her a bundle of cash bound in a dirty red rubber band and said "I'm pretty sure this will cover it."

I've never forgotten the look on the other salesmen's faces.

- *It is tough to love people with mental illness.*

This one startled me at first, but after a moment I figured it out. What I read in this remark is love, dedication, and commitment. How do you handle a situation where your loved one is fading away due to Alzheimer's disease? What if a parent suffers from manic depression? Or how is a child supposed to handle the fallout related to a parent being addicted to alcohol or drugs?

Children are incredibly resilient and resourceful, searching out support and companionship where they can find it. And when these children grow up, they easily recognize others who have suffered the same type of upbringing. They carry their battle scars close to the chest. But because they are a survivor of emotional neglect, they often create a solid foundation of strength from which they can stand to carve out their future.

If actions speak louder than words, I suggest that you make "transparency" a life goal; what is seen privately is the same behavior and attitudes the public observes. When you are consistent in your actions and thought processes, those who love you can more easily depend upon you. It's your very predictability that will create the stability in your relationships.

For example, I don't allow fish or seafood to be cooked in my house—I can't stand the smell or taste. If my husband chooses to eat seafood of any type, that day his efforts for any level of a romantic encounter will fail. So, his dilemma…when faced with a special seafood dinner or eating steak, he needs to consider how badly he wants affection that night. It's always his choice. My son cracks up when he dines with us and sees his father checking out the seafood side of the menu. He knows exactly the choice his father is making.

Life is about options and our selection process. In the next chapter, women open up and share the hardest decisions they ever had to make. Perhaps you will find the information will help you resolve a problem you are now facing…

Chapter Eight

The Family Connection

Families begin with a shared heritage, but they either grow close through adversity or they simply crumble apart. Have you ever seen a child throw a tantrum and then shake your head at the way the parent responded to the crisis? It's the weirdest feeling in the world...that lack of control. I've experienced the tantrum situation when my son was two years old and started a screaming fit in a toy department. He commanded attention from every passing mother, pleading his case for a new toy. His small grasping hands reaching out pitifully and clenched eyes with wide open mouth howling his dismay was almost enough to do me in. What kind of a mother would deny her beautiful baby what his heart desires?

Obviously...me.

Now, I had options. I could have gathered him up, tucked him under my arm—kicking and screaming and marched out of the store. But, doing that would have denied me the pleasure of finishing a much-needed shopping spree. So, I sat on the floor, placing myself at his eye level, and quietly waited for him to finish. A determined little bugger, he screeched his indignation for seven minutes, red faced, and tears streaking down his innocent cheeks. Other parents looked at me quickly, shared a brief smile of support, and moved to another aisle, hustling their children before them, hoping they don't get the same idea as my son's rebellion.

Do you have any idea how long seven minutes is with a shrieking child? A lifetime…

To this day, I don't know how I sat resolutely with a calm, patient expression on my face. The entire time, I pondered if my denial of his object of desire would destroy my relationship with my son. Will he sit in a psychoanalyst's chair as an adult and then blame me for his uncontrollable shopping urges? Isn't that the way it goes: children accusing their parents for all of the things that go wrong in their lives?

Figuring out exactly what our role is in a family can be tricky. We are more than disciplinarians; women are also the designated guardian of family traditions. Designated by whom, I have no idea. However, we know the devil is in the details and managing those intricate matters is what we do best. But regardless of our best efforts, sometimes the personalities of the family members are just too diverse to create a cohesive group.

Sadly, my relationship with my siblings has been splintered for years. Growing up with an older sister, a twin brother and twin sisters younger than I, I ended up exactly in the middle of the birth order. Responsibility ruled my oldest sister as she helped my parents with the kids, a burden that no seven-year-old should have to shoulder. Unwittingly, my mother had my oldest sister duplicate her upbringing by being responsible for the children.

My brother, being the only other male in the home besides my father, created his own social network and carved out his existence alone. My younger twin sisters needed no one else, their bond so complete that trying to pierce that barrier proved to be impossible.

And there I sat—disconnected and by necessity, self-reliant. With that solitude, I learned to appreciate my own company and sought avenues to express myself through music, writing, and reading. Longing to be part of something greater than myself, I gravitated to team sports like swim team, basketball and golf. In addition, I had intense connection with two people through my high school years and as a result, created my own surrogate family support system. They remain a valuable touchstone for me years later and with them, I learned the true meaning and value of connection. Aware of the issues I grew up with, I was curious what other women perceived as important in order to build a strong, positive family that stays connected and what causes them to crumble apart.

■ What does it take to build a strong, positive family that stays connected?

The responses to the question on building a strong family hold great power for me. I've chosen the top six responses in terms of frequency. Perhaps you will see something you can relate to…

- *Communication—keeps all issues out in the open.*

- *Unconditional love.*

- *Shared experiences—meals, fun, and reunions—quality time together.*

- *Stay connected—dedication to each other.*

- *Respect.*

- *Forgiveness. People act as best they can at the moment given the circumstances.*

I believe there are polar opposite ways of thinking about family life and typically people will fall into one camp or the other. Some people prefer to frame their experiences in terms of a great adventure and they embrace the positive impact their families have on their lives. Others find it easier to focus intensely upon the negative aspect of familial relationships they've survived, and they will be forever colored by that experience.

My parents had a tumultuous relationship filled with intense discussions. I was used to an environment where it was okay to be aggressively vocal in speaking my mind. However, when I met Rick's family, heated discussions didn't exist. As a result, one of my greatest fears was that my husband would leave me for another woman who was soft-spoken and genteel—qualities that I don't possess. There wasn't a logical reason for this fear; it had everything to do with my insecurity. In reality, it had nothing to do with him actually leaving me, but *how* he would possibly leave me. So we promised each other that if we ever did decide that we needed someone different in our lives, all we had to do was tell the other person, pack our bags, and leave *before* we started up with anyone else. It boiled down to having respect for each other as human beings. If he leaves in this manner, will it hurt any less? Of course not, but at least I won't have to worry about what others say or know before I did.

■ What do you believe destroys the unity of a family?

Part of knowing what makes a strong relationship is recognizing when the connection isn't there. The list below actually pinpoints behaviors that will destroy just about any type of relationship. My respondents identified that "blood is thicker than water," doesn't mean that a relative with a toxic personality must be forgiven unconditionally. People have to earn the right to be part of our lives and that includes family members. And the reverse is also true; we have to earn the right to be part of theirs.

- *Lack of constructive communication—deceit, lies and dishonesty that destroys trust*

- *Self-absorption: selfishness, greed and self-indulgence that relate to ego*

- *Disengagement by parents and between family members or not physically spending time together due to a geographical disconnect*

- *Disrespect: secrets, gossip about other family members*

- *Alcohol (or other substance abuse)*

- *Negative emotions: bitterness, jealousy, anger*

Even though my brother is my twin, our connection has never been intensely close in terms of ongoing contact. We know the essence of each other, so distance or time doesn't diminish the love we have as siblings. We each have built strong independent family units that replenish our emotional needs. With just a quick note or phone call, the distance evaporates.

Staying connected in a meaningful way with those who matter most in your life is a worthwhile objective. Many of the responses to this question will give you food for thought on forging the best relationships with your family.

Regardless of the relationship dynamics that exist in my family, if a sibling calls out for help, I'll respond. But, if I find I can't count on them when it really matters, I'm going to nurture strong personal relationships with people that are important to me. I don't intend on departing this earth alone. I want my family with me, either the one I was born into or the one I create.

In the end, it's ultimately up to me to define my family.

Chapter Nine

Life-Altering Decisions

I don't think any of us like to feel judged. But, I also believe it comes naturally to us to judge. We evaluate another person's decisions and then can't seem to withhold our opinion as to how we would have handled the same situation. We forget that all of us are simply human, trying to do the best we can on this earth. We shouldn't have to apologize for our parent's decisions or have unreasonable expectations placed on us because of the bounty we've been born to. Success and failure should be something we address on our own terms.

Nice fantasy.

Celebrities know what it's like to live under a microscope. Every misstep recorded for unending replay on YouTube.com. People seem to relish uncovering the "dirt" and then continue to scratch at the information like it's a scab. All of us have events we've buried in the past. Good—that's where it belongs. What relevance does a decision made as a freshman in high school have to do with us as a fifty-year-old business professional? Is our character ultimately judged upon stupid acts as a young adult?

How and where are we supposed to learn? With the scrutiny of today's media on obsessing about an individual's background, there's danger of information being taken out of context. When judgment starts, a whole new chain of events begins as the poor target tries to figure out how to get their life back.

Take Alaska's Sarah Palin, 2008 Republican Vice Presidential Candidate. Flung into the national spotlight, she struggled to find her footing. How could she keep her hometown roots secure and family intact while dealing with the onslaught of curiosity from the nation? Her life was dissected because the public wanted to know everything about her. The nation responded to her directness with delight, finally feeling a "real person" was running for the oval office.

The problem is, eventually perfection tarnishes. If you keep rubbing hard enough, flaws appear. Couple that with unprecedented attacks on her integrity as a political figure, woman, wife and mother, it got ugly. In 2009 she resigned from her position as Alaska's governor and stepped out of the limelight.

The responses to the following question, "what is the hardest decision you have ever made?" floored me with their intense honesty and insightful observations. As you read through the complete set of comments in the Appendix, you can almost visualize the pain and anguish a person faced making the decision that they did. With a startling number of similar responses, its evident these women are reaching out to others and letting them know they aren't alone.

■ What is the hardest decision you ever had to make?

Each of us goes through our own personal battles. With this question, I honor the war women have endured in their private way and the resources they relied upon to survive. The responses say it all.

- *Staying with my husband when I was about to 'have a breakdown' over his different views, based on his culture, on morality—there were several factors that played into my decision to finally leave. The first was my health from all of the anxiety. I was having heart palpitations and felt terrible and anxious all of the time. I don't know if this was because I had anxiety about the direction the relationship was heading or my husband's on-line and physical "fooling around." The other HUGE factor for me was watching a colleague's husband pass away from cancer. They had not made it to their first wedding anniversary. They were so in love and he was such a wonderful man. When I spoke with her about my situation, she told me to not waste any time being unhappy or settling. Families rebuild and they are stronger when everyone is in a positive and healthy state.*

- *Divorce, I had to sit back think of the ramifications of living with two children at a five-dollar-an-hour job. Talking with friends who knew what my husband had put me through for eighteen years. I would not have to be afraid anymore of being punched in the face or have a gun pulled on me. So many other horrid things he did to me...*

- *To admit to being an alcoholic and handle it by getting treatment and staying sober.*

- *Stop radiation & chemo and letting my husband go.*

- *Putting my mother in a nursing home and understanding that I could not do it by myself.*

- *Telling the doctor not to operate on my dad after his second massive heart attack in two days. I knew that if he was not able to live life the way he had before surgery, being able to be out in the woods hunting or on the water fishing, if he would be confined to his bed the rest of his life, he would hate me. The doctor told me that his chances of having a normal life were slim to none. I knew Dad did not want a life hooked up to machines, as much as I wanted him here with me.*

- *Forgiving my mother for an affair when I was a young child.*

- *To speak to my father after fifteen years of him saying to others outside the family that he had no children—I was an only child.*

- *Forgiving my mother—I realized that if I did not forgive my mother for not loving me the way that I needed to be loved, I would continue to give my power to her and would continue to play the "blame" and "victim" cards. I finally learned to love myself without needing it from others.*

- *Going to a therapist when I clearly needed to.*

- *Leaving a job I liked and was good at due to an irrational boss.*

- *Leaving a company that I had built from the ground up but that had lost its integrity and focus.*

- *Having a baby at a young age.*

- *To carry a child that was destined to be deformed.*

- *Not to have children—always too much of a career person.*

- *To put a baby up for adoption by trying to look to the future for him.*

- *Letting our wayward teenager go; we were in a battle of wills. A therapist said we had a 50/50 chance she would eventually live life based on the values she was raised with.*

- *To report my daughter's marijuana.*

- *To keep going after the death of my four-month-old with the help of my four-year-old son because he kept reminding me that Easton was always beside me in spirit and that no matter what, he and all my family still needed me.*

- *Putting down a pet with separation anxiety (and otherwise healthy and happy).*

As I review these answers, it brings to mind a trip that consisted of several epiphanies for me. My day started out innocently enough. The front desk remembered my 4:00 a.m. wake up call, the shower temperature was perfect, and the airport shuttle arrived on time. Check-in at the ticket counter proceeded without any waits or hitches. The clerk even took the time to joke with me. Wandering through the concourse, I purchased a couple of magazines that really interested me and received a great compliment on my stylish glasses. All this before 6:30 a.m! I relished the thought of an uneventful day.

I didn't expect to see a man collapse onto the hard tile floor as he emerged from the men's room.

In one moment, a perfectly groomed, sixty-year-old businessman had his day ripped away from him without advance notice. His confident stride, terminated. There was no stumble or stagger. He simply dropped to the floor, loose and unconscious. Sitting about twenty-five feet away, I and the other passengers could hear the back of his head bounce off the tile.

For two frozen seconds, no one reacted. Then humanity confirmed my belief in the goodness that resides in us all.

A frenzied scream "Jim!" erupted from a petite woman's mouth as she surged toward the men's room doorway. Five other men rushed after her, shouting to the clerk in the convenience shop to call 911. The explosion of activity centered on this trauma silenced every individual at the boarding gate.

For ten minutes, at least forty people held their breath, offering silent support to this woman who obviously was the man's wife. The airport security and medical staff arrived on the scene within six minutes…to find that the injured man had recovered consciousness and was mumbling. As I boarded the airplane, a gurney arrived and preparations were underway to transport the individual to a medical facility. I finally let out my breath.

Seeing the face of that woman as she leaped to her feet will stay with me for a very long time. Shock, disbelief, and utter despair rippled across her features as her skin turned a ghastly pale white. For a brief moment, I had feared for her as well.

In just a second, a completely uneventful day shattered with the unexpected. It seemed that this day's message was to be delivered over and over again.

Later that day in the Denver airport, I heard a baby's cry from across the airline terminal. Piercing the air, insistent and demanding, it didn't quite sound like an infant's voice. Curious, I looked around until I noticed a tired looking woman, patiently feeding yogurt into the mouth of the child, who was hidden behind a bumper pad in an oversized stroller. Pausing for a moment, the mother drank gratefully from a Starbucks coffee cup and our eyes briefly locked onto one another. An attitude of resignation floated around her—almost palpable in the air-conditioned space.

As I approached, I peered into the stroller. My heart skipped a beat.

A small person lay in the stroller…no more than three feet long. Small, womanly hands grasped at the napkin tucked into a pink sweater. Long brown hair fell in disarray on the bumper pad and pillow. The adult sized nose and large wandering eyes were in complete disproportion to the small chiseled cheekbones and jaw line. Another cry of impatience erupted once again from the gaping mouth filled with mature teeth, yet the mouth was no larger than one you would expect to see in a six-month baby.

Constantly scraping portions of yogurt which oozed from the small person's mouth, the mother whispered words of comfort to the flailing girl.

Time stopped for me.

As I sat down, I glanced around the gate area and spotted three other mothers hugging and playing with their small daughters—toddlers all. Flushed little cheeks, small legs skipping happily up and down the aisles and the tender hugs signified the absolute joy these children had in just being alive. I glanced back at the stroller and felt my heart break for this woman, isolated from life's simple joys.

Her child will never run, talk, or interact normally with her caretakers. Yet, her mother's words of comfort, whispered in a busy public place, seemed to be uttered almost like a talisman against all that is bad in the world. The routine, so practiced and normal, becomes a safe haven for them both.

Suddenly, I noticed a middle-aged man walking slowly toward the row of seats directly in front of me. His broad hand roughly massaged the back of his neck as he drank deeply a Red Bull energy beverage. It wasn't his gait or his obvious attempt to revive himself that caught my attention, but his tearing eyes and quivering lower lip.

The distraught man settled down in his seat and glanced nervously around. The entire time, I had the impression he was going to burst into tears, convinced that something terrible had happened to him or was about to happen.

Do I get up and offer comfort or give him the privacy he so desperately sought in a very public place? Torn and uncertain what to do, I remained seated.

Then, out of nowhere, an older gentleman with a leathery wrinkled face, stooped shoulders and a soft smile, settled into the seat next to the grieving man. As I watched, he leaned over, tapped the younger man on the shoulder and said quietly, "How are things going, big guy?" Startled, the other man's face flushed red, his lower lip trembled and a single tear ran down his cheek. The older man nodded his head and whispered, "I'll be happy to listen if you want to talk. Or, if you prefer, just sit with you for a while." A quiet companionship bloomed between strangers, generated by a person who had room to help shoulder someone else's burden, even if it was for only a short time.

I sighed, humbled and grateful for having witnessed this simple kindness.

As the wise women we are, we realize that all of the personal and family issues we've experienced are transitory... they had a beginning and will have a foreseeable end. The tired mother with the genetically wounded child must face each day with bravery and strength, if not for her, then for her child. She knows what the morning will bring and she still gets up—over and over again.

Who knows what the story is for the person who weeps publically because something so powerful has overwhelmed their senses? Whether generated from loss, fear, or part of a mental illness, we will never know. The demons are their own and somehow must be addressed and resolved—but only if their hearts can stand the strain of rising up to the challenge.

This question, and the respondents' deeply honest answers, really caused me to reflect on my toughest decision: to trust my husband beyond all doubt. By the time I met Rick, all I knew was people turned on you when you least expected it, emotionally and physically. I'd developed a hard emotional overcoat and really didn't want to relinquish control to another person ever again.

Then he embraced me for who I was, what I stood for, what I believed in, and where I wanted to go. Raised to believe I wasn't good looking, my husband never wavers in his belief that I'm an incomparable beauty, inside and out. Patiently, he waited years for me to hand over control and now that he has it, he guards that trust with a gentle yet ferocious hand. He is my champion.

This chapter focuses on the decisions we've had to make which impacted our life direction. We know the "what" and "whys"; below I've listed some suggestions to help you with the "how" to make decisions an easier process for you:

- Learn about how others make life-altering decisions: whom do they talk to and whom do they rely upon. I've learned that decisions made alone are more painful than when I have a trusted confidante I can run things by.

- Forfeit multi-tasking when it comes to your relationship with your best friend, husband, or child. In just a second, they could be gone from your life and you should refuse to have regrets about how your lives were lived.

- Think about your life and those individuals who give you joy. What would you think if they were no longer in your life and what would you wish you would have told them? How would you have wished you had lived your life?

- Quit wishing and take action. Do something now so that when a life-changing moment comes…you won't have regrets.

Our lives are the only ones we are going to get and the prospects are just too rich to ignore. With that in mind, let's explore what we would do differently if we did have that magic wand. The next chapter gives us a chance to consider changes to our lives that will enrich our experiences and relationships.

Chapter Ten

Second Chances

I began this book talking about how we don't get "do-overs" in life. But that doesn't mean that we can't learn from our mistakes—look at what we could have done differently so we don't do the same stupid thing again. And, as I have been hinting at all along, it's always good to listen to others. It's never too late to make a constructive change. All it takes is one idea or recommendation to make a large difference in your life.

In past generations, the elders held a treasured status within the family structure and community. The knowledge they gained from their vast life experiences became a guide for their children, essentially clearing the path for a richer fuller human experience.

At some point, the term "old" became a dirty word. I'm guilty of being upset when the AARP card appeared in my mail. I ripped the letter into tiny pieces and declared loudly, "I'm not a Senior Citizen yet!" My husband smiled knowingly like the Cheshire cat from the Alice in Wonderland story.

What good is a life lived if the people you care about most don't bother to listen to your sage advice and counsel? Sure, some of our home remedies might be ridiculous (i.e. remember the scene in the movie My Big Fat Greek Wedding where the father uses Windex to cure all ills?) But what about the message from parents who survived the Great Depression where they advised us to not outlive our means and only buy something when you could pay cash in order to avoid going into debt?

If more children had listened to that advice, the housing debacle that began in 2007 might have been avoided. With a nation more deeply in debt, our regret of not having listened falls on deaf ears as we diligently work to bail ourselves out of the situation.

Our children have lessons they can teach us every day. We raised them to be fiercely independent, to utilize the resources available to them, and to step fearlessly into their futures. This younger generation relentlessly seeks ways to connect with people and share experiences worldwide. Instead of observing with amazement, why not join them?

■ What is the one thing you would do differently in your life?

Really, what good is wisdom if we can't share it with others? That is the purpose of asking this question. Perhaps it might be possible to consider what has been shared in order to help us make our life decisions a bit easier. I've chosen to comment on only a few of the answers. Read on and maybe you will find elements that resonate with you.

- *I would not have had children. God doesn't have a return policy.*

   I was startled to read this answer. As a mom, I instinctually thought about the children and what their lives may have been like, living with a woman who didn't want them. Then, upon reflection, I realized that this was an incredibly brave thing to write. This doesn't mean she wasn't a good mother; it could be that she put her potential and dreams aside to raise a family and help them succeed. She may have lived vicariously through her offspring. Or perhaps her kids have created such stress and anxiety for her, that at some point a person has to give up. Until we have a frame of reference, it's impossible to judge.

But it does make us think about the role children play in our lives.

- *We're losing tradition, we don't eat together. The time you spend with your children defines who they will turn out to be. Understanding that family is the most important thing in the world, I passed the responsibility off to babysitters.*

Here is where that old argument rears its ugly head; what is best for our children—quality time or quantity time? Not all women are hardwired to be stay-at-home Moms. It doesn't mean they don't love their children. Convinced that my son needed to have a happy mother, I entered the workforce when he was an infant and never looked back. Would he have been a different child if I stayed home? Who knows? But then, maybe I wouldn't have the wonderfully gentle, dedicated loving son I have now if I had. It's too close to call.

- *I was taught as a child to take care of others first! It is still a hard thing for me to put myself first, but I have become better at it the older I am. Unfortunately, at age sixty, my options are becoming less.*

As women, we are naturally nurturing and easily assume the role of caretaker. But for how long do we keep ourselves in that role? Perhaps at age sixty this woman has done her time (sounds like a prison sentence). Ladies, we always have options—limited only by our health and mental agility. Step out of fear and look for the opportunities that will give you the personal satisfaction you've earned.

- *I needed more patience. I think that it would have helped our son to make better decisions in his life.*

How can we be held responsible for the choices our children make? Who placed that burden on our shoulders and why did we accept that? At some point, we should realize that our kids are not an extension of our own being. They develop their own interpersonal skills, dream their dreams, and make decisions based upon their personal experiences. Our children get into trouble, either at school, with friends or possibly with the law. When we broadcast our pure mortification, it registers on every sympathetic mother's heart.

All we can do is pack the lunch, give them a kiss, teach them that actions have consequences, and hope they walk the right path. At some point we have to recognize that we have done what we could and let go.

These next comments were wonderful. To me, they shout satisfaction and contentment—an emotional state we all strive to achieve as early as possible in our lives…

- *Learn to accept and forgive myself for who I was at a much earlier age; wisdom comes with age but we need it so much sooner in life. That realization would have made my life so much easier and more enjoyable. Instead of trying to live up to certain standards or what I thought others wanted me to be I would have been more comfortable in my skin, not tried to impress others or cared so much about what they thought I think. I am more "myself" now and I care less if others judge me. My new motto: be who you are and say what you feel, because those that matter don't mind and those that mind don't matter.*

- *I believe that every single second of my life has led to the place where I am right now. I am deeply, truly happy and would not change a thing because I am where I am because of my past decisions.*

- *I wouldn't change anything because I would not look the same, act the same, or have "my" unique character traits and beliefs that make me who I am.*

I have to agree wholeheartedly with these statements. Regret serves no purpose and it changes nothing. I recently cleaned out a cabinet stuffed with old photographs of our family. I had a great time laughing at my husband's image from thirty years ago, but a sense of wonder came over me as I scrutinized a picture of me at the age of thirty-five. I had cheek bones, a flawless complexion and an aristocratic profile. The look of complete love on my face as I wrapped my arms around my ten year old son turned me to mush. When I gazed upon that youthful image, I realized that I may not be able to return to that age, but I sure could work hard to ensure my body enters this next stage as healthy as possible.

Even though society emphasizes youthful vibrancy as something we should strive for, it is a reality that we have bodies that are going to betray us. The message from these women is not to lament what we can't have but to appreciate what we have learned, such as:

- We are no longer naïve.
- We have learned the power of one voice.
- We are survivors.
- Our years on this earth have sculpted us into the individuals we are today. Each experience is fully revealed on the final masterpiece of our maturity.

- It takes aging to develop a sense of humor, purpose and an appreciation for the power of personal dignity. There's a calmness and certainty we possess now that we wouldn't trade for anything in order to regain the tumultuous years of our twenties.

If you feel your life is filled with regrets, I suggest that you identify the things you can actually fix and then work actively to resolve them. You have plenty of years left in you to make a new life for yourself based upon the dreams and expectations of what you want.

As for those things you can't fix or resolve, write them down on a piece of paper. Then burn them. It's not only a visual stimulus to see these regrets go up in smoke and dissipate into the air, but you can also cook marshmallows and make S'mores.

We may be getting older, but by God, we've never been better. This is really evident in the comments I received regarding career challenges women have faced over the years. By reading the next chapter, you may find out that you aren't alone in the workplace; that the woman working alongside you may very well be thinking the same thing you are.

Chapter Eleven

Career Challenges

Quite frankly, it feels weird to be on the downward slope of our careers. At least, that is what a twenty-eight year recently said to me. At a younger age, the thought of retiring seemed like a distant prospect. Now, in my mid fifties, I'm actually checking out my Social-Security statement to confirm how much money I may have to work with if I do end up leaving the workforce. As we age, we perceive time to be going by much more quickly, and we have no clue as to how to slow things down.

We've already acknowledged that the world of technology has moved to a different level than what we have been used to working with. Along with that realization is the inevitable fact that corporate executives will need and search for those employees who embrace and are competent in societal changes.

Where does that leave us? It depends upon your attitude, how effective you were in creating a powerful cadre of relevant knowledge that the company values and appreciates, and your willingness to adapt to new, high-speed ways of accomplishing your projects. Think about it from an employers point of view: we are the most expensive employees for an organization with tenure creeping us up to the top of the payroll range; we utilize most of the medical benefits; and we run the risk of possibly being known as having an attitude of "what happened?" vs. "what's next."

In the corporate world, I believe it's critical, as women, that we discuss how we can transition to new expectations for our lives by visualizing what is important to us, our families and our wellbeing—emotionally and physically.

We will be confronted continually with others on the job not listening to our advice and frustration is bound to increase. There is nothing more aggravating than trying to help someone and they won't listen. The reality is they may have already figured out the solution and are using a technology you didn't even know existed. If you think we feel blindsided, imagine what people in their eighties are thinking!

At no time in our national history have we had as many generations in the workforce as today. That issue alone creates a huge possibility of disconnect and miscommunication. If we are perceived as being on the downward slope, then why would they put us in key positions? Personally, I believe this is why many women have begun their own home-based businesses in areas like real estate, employment contractual services, or as consultants.

Our biggest challenge is to refresh our outlook at how we perceive our contribution to the workforce. The younger generations of women know about the freedom of individual expression and have a complete confidence in their abilities. We did that for them by tackling sexual discrimination head-on and stepping up our game to compete in a man's environment. What doesn't kill us makes us stronger, right? Our daughters will face a different set of corporate directives than we did because we now live in a global environment, not national. There are no more borders.

Some of us don't do really well without defined boundaries. But we better get used to it because our children toppled that inhibition at a very early age. I asked the question, "What are the top challenges you face in your work or career?" to confirm my perception that the work environment is much better for women, but I found that peer-to-peer issues continue to create havoc at the office.

■ What are the top challenges you face in your work or career?

What is interesting is that the women who responded to the survey identified a wide variety of challenges mostly related to the work environment and tasks. As I summarized their responses; twenty areas surfaced as common concerns about workplace challenges and are listed in the Appendix. Below are the most intriguing to me.

- *Lack of respect for my career abilities and competing in a male-dominated environment.*

  I've observed such unprofessional behavior from women that it made me cringe. We work in a man's world and hopefully our daughters are adapting more readily to the work environment than we did. In a man's world, the corporate environment is about:

  - ¤ Pragmatic decision-making processes
  - ¤ Linear thinking
  - ¤ Skillful politicking
  - ¤ Networking with purpose
  - ¤ Strategic planning
  - ¤ Direct interpersonal communication—a directive is given, it is expected to be followed

Women, however, build relationships first, working to establish rapport and common goals. These can be powerful skills in the workplace if utilized properly. However, there have been times I felt the women I worked with have been totally clueless…let me share with you an extreme example:

I hired a lovely young woman for a clerical position. In the interview, she arrived impeccably dressed and interacted with me in a highly professional manner. On her first day, one week later, she arrived at the office and stopped traffic when she stepped off the elevator. The phone extensions started ringing down the corridor as if ushering her to her desk. She stepped into my office and said perkily, "I'm ready to get to work!"

My jaw hit the table as I stared at her see-through black blouse and naked bosoms; nothing left to the imagination. I tossed my jacket to her and instructed her to put it on. Her look of sheer bafflement remains with me today. She refused to cover up saying "If you have it, why not flaunt it?" Needless to say, she never did make it back to her desk. The situation ended being a joke at my expense for months in my department.

We encounter many stereotypes in our office environment. For some women, work is a way to meet men. Unfortunately the flirting and romantic repartee wears thin on the other employees. And for others, work becomes a safe haven where they can retreat when their home life becomes unstable. Then there have been women who consider the office cubicle much like the fence that divides properties in a neighborhood—an invitation for socializing.

Or we can address another stereotype—the office bitch. What comes to your mind when you read this? I think of a woman who is focused, knows what she wants, won't back down when she knows she is right, and isn't easily intimidated by men. She feels she has a right and a duty to use her brains for the betterment of the task at hand and if she also happens to be a classy dresser as well...all I can say is "Wow." Typically, this type of woman doesn't have time for social chatter; they have a task to do and when it's done, they want to enjoy their personal life, thank you very much.

It's too bad that when a woman demonstrates the very skills that men are praised for, she is negatively labeled. And what is most sad of all, the label is often first uttered in the female camp.

Then there are the ladies who fit right in the middle. They don't forfeit femininity in order to be perceived as professional but embrace the knowledge they have to offer a company and find a path of engagement that works well for everyone.

- *Time management, organization and life balance between career and home life. Keeping up with technology which may ultimately make my job obsolete.*

Today's world is changing at an exponential speed. Just check out the video, "Did You Know," on YouTube.com and prepare yourself. We grew up in a world where paradigm shifts occurred once every thirty years. This term, coined by Thomas Kuhn in his book, *The Structure of Scientific Revolutions*, refers to how change challenges our basic assumptions in life. For example, how we adapted from horse-drawn carriages to automobiles—true shifts in perception and society development.

Today, we are experiencing paradigm shifts every three years. No wonder our heads are spinning. Are we moving forward so fast that we aren't taking time to consider the consequences of change? In our lifetime, the way we communicate, interact, and thrive as a society is fundamentally different than what we experienced as a child. Future soldiers are masters of warfare because they've been raised playing games in a virtual environment and future weaponry will be virtually driven. Has someone cloned a human being now that the kitten has been cloned perfectly? Is the concept of family evolving to a broader interpretation that doesn't include married spouses? Because the world is so flat, will a ripple of change thousands of miles away rip a hole in our reality?

It is human nature if we discover we can do something, we do it! What we may not consider is whether it's the right thing to do; the classic clash between technological advances and cultural/ethical beliefs. Take the new Star Trek movie. New recruits for starship duty are educated in individual pods operated electronically—no instructor but the voice of the computer and visual imagery flashing quickly to highlight a concept. Highly interactive, the student drives the education. What a different concept where we grew up with teachers creating a curriculum and staying the course for nine months. Student-driven education is a concept revolutionizing our method of instruction that now includes on-line training resources, teleseminars, webinars, and Wikis.

But you know what? I still think the fax machine is a miracle.

Webster's Dictionary describes change as making an essential difference in some particular aspect without suggesting loss of identity. That is how Baby Boomers like us fit into a high-tech world; adapting the good, bad, and ugly into our personal view of the world and taking action to incorporate change as a positive enhancement of how we already operate.

- *Women not helping other women succeed or backstabbing.*

This is one perception I hope to challenge as a result of this book. As a past Human Resource professional, I've had male managers laughingly state to me that they have to babysit the women who work for them. These comments were a poor attempt at a joke, but they meant it. I suffer from a pang of regret knowing that our reputation as corporate workers can be damaged by such a broad brush stroke.

An issue that is repeated continually in a work environment usually involves an individual doing a great job on a project, being recognized by upper-level management for that effort, and then they experience a backlash of resentment from their peers. Utilizing the term "brown nosing" is one way for people to bring down a rising star. Technically, it's emotional blackmail. When someone excels at a task, why do others immediately feel threatened rather than join in the richly deserved congratulations, especially if that individual truly expended an exceptional level of effort and did not tread on others to reach that success level?

I urge you to conduct a personal accountability inventory and be brutally honest in uncovering those areas you should improve in terms of working with other females in the department or company. Personally, I believe we are the architect of our achievements and if our foundation is weak, and we don't support our peers in striving to reach their personal objectives, attainment of our goals is unlikely.

Take a moment and think about what spurs you on. What do you need in order to move forward in achieving the objectives that are important to you? Maybe these parting thoughts might be of value to you:

- Though competition is a good thing if viewed in a healthy way, learn to focus on your individual accomplishments and don't worry about what other people are doing.

- Internalize your professional issues and work hard to develop emotional calm. Try to cut your anxiety in half.

- If you stop pushing for something and concentrate on how you can help others, good things will happen in your life. The concept of "what you give comes back to you tenfold," isn't just an old adage; it truly is a miracle that comes to a life lived in collaboration and support of others.

- Try to make one small change at a time—this can reinforce the intuition of a curious mind as you evaluate implications before you leap.

- Wake up each morning wondering what is next and love every moment.

Challenges are only part of the story. In the next chapter let's explore what impacts a work environment, negatively and positively.

Chapter Twelve

Business Hazard or Safety Zone?

Employee retention is one of the largest issues facing corporations today. With several generations in the workplace, trying to find a productive culture that entices in new blood without alienating the older employees proves to be a real challenge. Our daughters have more acceptance of their abilities by the work population, but with the younger generation's high-speed approach to life, it's harder to keep them engaged in work they find meaningful.

Imagine this scenario from an older person's traditional point of view: A meeting is ready to begin and everyone has their laptops open and fired up. Several other people are sending texts on their "smart" phones as Lattes from the local Starbucks outlet are passed around. Then the facilitator says, "I'll take your questions via Twitter. Just send your tweets as the meeting progresses, and they'll be displayed on my monitor. And by the way, Jason is with us on Skype, so be sure to speak up so he can hear you. Also, mark your calendars; we will be meeting virtually on Secondlife.com next Tuesday. I'll provide you with details at the end of this meeting. Welcome everyone!"

Gulp! Whatever happened to just bringing a note pad and pen, drinking from the communal coffee pot and simply raising a hand when a question came up? And what the heck is a virtual meeting? Why can't we meet in the conference room like we always have?

Now more than ever, our work environment is perfect for the way women communicate. With social networking on-line becoming so popular and sharing a common state of being, this is a coffee klatch magnified tenfold. We should be ecstatic! Our desire to connect at a more meaningful level is enhanced by technology, not hindered. Our children embraced technology and raised it to an art form in terms of communication between males and females. Because of this shift, people are evaluated more on the value of the information shared than the manner in which it is delivered.

Because of the onslaught of this information age, the people who will rise to the top in a corporate environment are those who can interpret the data and make connections that result in another perceptual shift. Where the problems arise is when younger people are hired by older individuals who refuse to acknowledge that our world is different. Our children might be told they have an "attitude" problem when they try to introduce new protocols or deliver the information in a 140-character tweet.

In reality, retention is an issue for management because our self-confident children will continue to search for a work environment that appreciates their contribution (loyalty only as good as long as they are paid appropriately for the work they do), and the work is engaging enough to keep them happy. They already understand that life is too short to be bored in their job.

The most disappointing thing about being self-employed and working alone is I have no one to blame for a negative work environment. If my attitude suffers, so does my company.

Essentially, I must motivate myself, which has proven to be easier than motivating some employees.

As individuals, we hold great power in formulating a positive environment. It is crucial that supervisors and managers understand the impact of their personality on others and how it can either enhance or detract from a positive career experience. In search of collaborative feedback, I felt it was critical to ask the respondents, "What does it take to build a strong, positive work environment as well as what destroys a culture?" Perhaps armed with this information, we can really make a difference in our approach to work and how we relate to those who toil right alongside us.

■ What does it take to build a strong, positive work environment?

From the survey answers, I've isolated a few statements to discuss. Read on to learn about the opinions of career women and maybe you might find that magic wand to repair your broken culture or improve the exceptional one you already have nurtured.

- *Strong, uplifting leaders who support their employees by listening, having the courage to make and back up tough decisions, act with enthusiasm, and are fair in their treatment of employees.*

We want and need heroes—those individuals who give us hope and can rouse people to move forward toward a common goal. Consider this scenario:

Dawn is arriving. The chilly air causes the breath of the waiting mass of humanity to materialize as briefly hanging ghostly shapes. Twilight recedes as the sun slowly ascends over the horizon, spearing the darkness with the brilliant light of hope and promise of a new day where anything can happen. Crisp aroma of meadow flowers fills the air and the crowd inhales deeply to capture the scent, if only for a moment.

They wait.

Suddenly, the quiet is shattered by the hammering of a majestic horse's hooves as it gallops over the crest of the hill. Backlit by the rising sun, the anointed leader surges into view and a mighty cheer erupts from the crowd, deafening in the celebration of their chosen leader. Raising a hand, asking for quiet attention, the leader guides the prancing steed, resplendent in silver and highly polished leather, up and down the front lines looking deeply into the eyes of those who have chosen to follow.

After the intense moment of connection, the leader positions the horse at a location where every eye can see him and the sound of the leader's voice carries easily to every woman, man, and child gathered in the meadow.

Eyes flashing, head held high, he speaks.

The voice of authority, possibility, love, and urgency fills the air and those who listen feel their eyes fill with tears, too enraptured to hold back any emotion. This is the day when we fight for our freedom.

Independence Day.

At least that is how the movies and books say leadership looks and feels. This rousing, intense interaction between leader and follower is natural and logical; but, let's re-run the scenario again for today's environment:

Twilight is arriving. All company employees move quickly into the corporate lobby. Through the rain streaked windows, employees witness the sun as it descends behind the skyline, obscured by smog. A day is ending, where each employee knows anything can happen. The smell of panicked sweat permeates the air.

They wait.

Suddenly, the murmur of the assembly is shattered by the elevator door opening one story above at the atrium level. Backlit by the florescent light, the president of the company calmly walks up to the railing and looks down over the crowd. Raising a manicured hand, asking for quiet attention, the leader, looking tired and pale, gazes sadly into the eyes of those who have been hired to work for her company.

Choosing a location at the railing where every eye can see her, the sound of the leader's voice carries easily to every woman and man. The voice of authority and urgency fills the air and those who listen feel their eyes fill with tears, too shocked to hold back emotion. This is the day when they are given their freedom—released from their jobs due to the recession.

Independence Day.

Both scenarios highlight a leader who can stand and deliver the best and worst of news with compassion and strength. Harsh, necessary decisions are the responsibility of a leader and delivering the results of those decisions to members who are following you with trust and commitment is one of the hardest things a leader will ever do.

I believe that is why fewer women are willing to assume the mantle of leadership, even if it only involves personal responsibility.

Leadership is placed on our shoulders in all sorts of ways: group acclimation, recognition of a job well done, or as a logical progression in the scheme of things. Often we receive the benefit of ascension to a position of power through financial rewards, perks, public recognition, and the ability to create necessary change. That has to sustain us at night when we have trouble sleeping.

Often, many leaders feel isolated because they choose to keep power and information firmly within their grasp, afraid that any leak of bad data would cause anxiety in the workforce and negatively impact productivity. Isn't the leader supposed to be strong enough to stand alone?

Let's go back to the movie scenario. This leader exudes confidence in his followers, an undying faith that they will understand the issues at hand, and work with him to solve the problem through group interaction—even if that means charging down a path to a destination that could result in destruction. At least they did it together.

The role of the leader isn't about isolation. It's about creating such a powerful presence within a group that people choose to follow you, knowing their voices will be heard, considered, and implemented when it makes sense. The members believe in the direction the leader is taking, have faith in the outcome, and willingly give up their independence for a greater good.

The power of leadership is in collaboration. When that happens, anything is possible, even in the harshest of times.

- *Provide opportunities for cooperation, collaboration—allow and encourage creative freedom and risk taking.*

I believe women connect more easily and at a deeper personal level with other women than men do with each other. The sheer speed in which we interact emotionally is a strength we should continue to treasure, especially when those connections are genuine and authentic.

The power of several minds working on a project can be exhilarating. When leadership is confident in its collective ability, creating an environment for creative problem solving seems to evolve naturally. In reality, strong people don't fear competition…instead they learn and assimilate new ideas into current ways of thinking.

- *Work with each employee's strengths rather than focus on the negatives—praising people to success.*

Through numerous personnel evaluations I've received for work done in a corporate environment, most of the feedback concentrated on the negatives of my performance. Regardless of whether my overall review was excellent or not, the majority of the conversation with my managers centered upon those areas I could "tweak."

I'm sick of tweaking.

For one manager, inevitably, a skill might be perceived as needing improvement, another manager would declare my level of ability in that skill set to be a well received strength. The more reviews I had, the more confused I became. Finally, I realized that I couldn't satisfy everyone. All I could do was concentrate on the task I'd been charged with and make the best effort possible to meet the goals and objectives of the position and organization.

Later, in my role as a human-resource manager, I changed the emphasis of the evaluation format for my direct reports. Preferring to build on their individual strengths, I expended my energies on supporting skills they excelled at. I realized their strengths were what kept my department running smoothly. Concentrating on deficiencies can end up being counter-productive; as the employee's anxiety increases while they try to "fix" a skill set they don't really care about, morale will probably plummet.

■ What do you believe destroys the culture of a business?

- *Micro-managing employees—no room for people to be creative.*

My best managers have been the people who gave me tasks to complete and then left the details as to how I did it up to me. Women are extremely good at details because that is what we do daily; balancing our home and work lives. We continually create plans of action in our heads as we coordinate schedules while running at full speed.

This is exactly why it is harder for a woman to delegate to others. We know what we can do and we also know that it will be done right if we do it ourselves. In the corporate world, if effective teams aren't built and nurtured, women will fail in the management role. It's as simple as that.

- *Management not staying on top of what goes on with workers—limited commitment to employees.*

One of my favorite sayings is, "You never know what another person is experiencing until you walk a mile in their shoes." Isolation from the actual work performed by subordinates seems to be a nasty trend. When workers begin to think a leader can't relate to what they're experiencing, communication ceases. I recommend that you sit for a day individually with all of your direct reports and learn about the tasks they do. A few things will be accomplished:

1. You'll get to know the employee on a more personal level;

2. An understanding of how work is conducted is achieved;

3. Communication is easier as you will erase the "ivory tower" mentality when they recognize your value as part of the team.

I never said it wouldn't take work.

I find it interesting that, to me, the survey respondents' interpersonal issues were predominant over specifics such as unfair pay, lack of raises, or minimal vacation time. What this tells us is the connection between management and staff is critical to a healthy environment. Women need to believe that what they offer to their company is appreciated on a personal level.

Keeping your focus on the employee in terms of improving processes seems like a logical place to put your attention. By interacting with purpose, you can insure that your direct reports understand the goals and mission of the company they work for. For all intents and purposes, you are the company. And who you are is more important to them than what you do.

As leader in your company, from the moment you walk in the door early in the morning to the last few moments as you exit for the return trip home, the attitude and general wellbeing of the employees need to take precedence over your own issues.

That's a heavy burden to bear, but the rewards in employee commitment will make it worth it.

Whether you are a non-exempt employee or an officer of a company, these reminders will have value for you:

- The simple act of connecting at a level that matters increases an employee's commitment toward better performance and keeps them engaged in the objectives of the company.

- Instead of giving a customary company coffee mug to an employee on their tenth anniversary of employment, why not investigate what that person really enjoys doing on their off hours and reward them with something they actually value.

- Create multiple opportunities for group interaction and problem solving.

- Build upon employee strengths to increase engagement and commitment.

- Allow your staff to take risks. There is a freedom that comes with the possibility of failure. Without risk, some of the greatest discoveries may not have happened.

- Stay in touch with how your employees do their jobs to enhance communication and understanding.

For managers, take the time to consider how you impact your work environment and work diligently to build something you are proud of. I believe the most important thing a corporate executive can do is work diligently to create a working environment that not only thrives on innovation, tackles change with a positive mindset, and encourages relevant input from the employees, but actually acts upon those recommendations whenever they make sense to do so.

For employees, understand how you contribute to the company's overall goals, objectives, and bottom line. If everyone isn't working toward those goals, it is possible your position will eventually not exist anymore. Take ownership in your professional growth. When you do that, others will notice.

In the end, the corporate culture is in the hands of everyone who works there. Make sure your imprint is a positive one.

Chapter Thirteen

Grateful for the Simple Things

We have gone on quite a journey through the last three chapters, exploring regrets, careers, and business cultures. All of these areas have influenced us and created the women we are today. Now is the time to "think forward" and to begin recognizing we are more in control of our lives than we thought possible. What follows in this book are those concepts that are as important in the workplace as they are in everyday life. By acknowledging the simple things that bring us joy, we can consciously fill ourselves with gratitude for a life well lived. It's about stopping the fast pace of our environment and truly seeing what is around us in order to determine the best path for our futures.

Meandering through the wonders of life such as the invention of indoor plumbing is enough to bring tears of gratitude to my eyes.

I rejoice in being alive in this century. I'd fail as a pioneer woman or a medieval serf. Early in my career as a REALTOR®, I met Hope who raised goats and rabbits on her property. Remembering the jumping antics of the baby goats is a cherished memory. I recall walking into her kitchen for our first appointment and observing her children playing with a white rabbit. Noticing the direction of my gaze, she swiveled to face her brood and declared firmly, "Kids…stop playing with dinner."

Blink. Was she serious?

Seeing my stricken face, Hope calmly explained that everything they raised was essential to the family, including the goats which provided milk and meat. Gulp.

I've decided that if a nuclear holocaust strikes the Midwest, I'll seek out Hope and her family and move in. At least I know someone with a pioneer spirit and independent lifestyle who will know how to feed me.

I'm conscious and grateful for really simple things. At least once a day, I inhale deeply, thinking how lucky I am to be able to breathe. Then I begin to marvel at the human body itself: its capacity to heal wounds, bloat beyond measure with water weight, and the mind's ability to design a computer or produce music or paint so clearly it almost looks like a photograph.

■ What do you rejoice in the most?

Let's explore what women find amazing in life. You'll probably be surprised to see how much there is to be grateful for…it's just a matter of perspective.

- *Volunteerism.*

  The simple act of raising our hand and offering to help is one of the most powerful things a human being can do. Acts of charity and kindness happen all around us each day, like my aunt delivering a plate of cookies to a new neighbor. A small gesture, yet it will have a lasting effect of goodwill. That is something that can't be bought.

  Some of us enjoy the benefits of belonging to an association. Part of a member's responsibility is to help make the organization as strong as possible. Your contribution doesn't have to require a huge time commitment; often a small task can prove to be a vital one to the association leadership.

Sometimes our calling to volunteer comes unexpectedly. My twin brother, Kevin, had worked in the computer software industry for most of his adult life—until the last few years. He and his wife, Chellie, now travel to Africa several times a year coordinating land purchases for the building of schools through their philanthropic fund. Seeing their faces light up when they show photos of their endeavors proves to me they are gaining much more than what they give personally.

- *In being heard.*

At a very young age, our son would wake up early in the morning and shuffle to my husband's side of the bed, the top of his tousled head barely showing above the mattress. Sleeping soundly, we'd awaken to a loudly whispered, "Dad."

If my husband didn't respond by opening his eyes, Ben would try again, louder, "Dad."

Sometimes, faking sleep, we'd wait to see what he would do. We couldn't contain our chuckles when we'd hear his disgusted grunt because we didn't react to his call. He would keep repeating, "Dad," until he was heard and acknowledged.

As adults, we do the same thing. We'll keep repeating ourselves until we feel we've been heard. It's a wonderful feeling when we don't have to do that—when the person we are speaking to is fully focused on us and appreciates what we have to say.

- *The spiritual awakening that is happening.*

For generations, people have searched their hearts and the heavens for greater meaning. Some gravitate to organized religion while others prefer to hold their spirituality privately. We are on a journey of discovery and the older we get, the more convinced many of us become that there are wonders that are waiting to be uncovered in this world.

Several years ago, while in England, I stood and stared at the mystic Stonehenge. Druids believed the region was a center of spiritual power. Was I supposed to receive an electric charge from the earth to let me know I stood in the shadow of greatness? I felt the wind, smelled the newly mowed grass, and enjoyed watching the mist as it drifted among the stones and wondered what really happened here and why.

I felt no surge of energy. And that was fine because I got something far more profound. Humility filled me as I appreciated the accomplishment of people who lived centuries before me. I felt reverence and that awakening is something I cherish.

This question "What do I rejoice in the most," prompted me to evaluate how I approached my life on a daily basis and whether I really do appreciate the simple things. I discovered something interesting—I honestly didn't know what to do with myself if I wasn't working. When I make time to "relax," all I can think about are the projects that require my attention—new ideas, strategic plans, and networking opportunities.

In reality, I believe I was just afraid of what might happen if I stopped.

J.J. Gordon said something interesting, "If we are to perceive all the implications of the new, we must risk, at least temporarily, ambiguity and disorder." It reminds me of a vacation we took to Lake Tahoe, Nevada. Trees, squirrels, water, and nature abounded in this beautiful retreat from an overloaded schedule—the perfect place to indulge in a personal time out.

I wasn't sure I could do it—sit still and do nothing. Forced to leave my computer behind (a command from my husband) I felt isolated and disconnected. Not checking my e-mail five times a day had become an ingrained habit; my fingers' phantom urgings to strike a computer key almost hurt. My husband insisted I enjoy the outdoors by relaxing at a picnic table near the azure blue lake. He wandered away to explore the shoreline. Sun sparkled off the calm surface and caressed my face. I began to think I could get used to this. Then the attack began.

A large yellow bumble bee swooped and dove around my head. Flailing arms and shoulder jerks only seemed to increase the persistent bee's interest in me. Shrieking, I dodged from pine tree, to rock, to the parking lot. It tracked me with the expertise and determination of Daniel Boone. I lunged to our car, yanked open the door, jumped in, and slammed the door. The predator bee landed on the driver's door mirror and stared at me through multifaceted eyes. It looked hungry.

I started the car and roared out onto the two-lane highway. That bee clung onto the mirror until the aero dynamics from a sixty-five-mile-an-hour speed limit sucked it away into the void behind the car. My cry of triumph still echoes throughout the Tahoe forest.

That simple act made me feel like a pioneer adventuring into the unknown wilderness. Out of the disorderly flight, I gained my composure and self-confidence. By the time I returned to my perch at Lake Tahoe, my incessant need to be in constant motion receded. That's when I finally got it.

As I sat on the log and gazed out over the water, I reveled in the startling blue color cutting a path through green verdant hills—serenity on earth. Quiet prevailed. Even the birds tittered softly as if respecting my need for solitude and reflection. Whoa! So this is what a mental time out feels like?

By appreciating the simple things in life, finding joy in as many places as possible, we can become the architect of our own health: mentally and physically. If we value true contentment, perhaps we might look up from our work and appreciate what we have at that moment.

It's all about the perspective on life we choose to have. It's the one thing we do have control over: such a simple thing, yet so powerful.

Chapter Fourteen

The Next Generation

We bring children into the world as a physical reminder of the love we share with another person and to gain a bit of immortality—hoping a new generation can accomplish those goals that we couldn't reach. And as parents, we really believe we can conquer the world or at the very least control outside negative influences.

But, we never believed it could happen to us. We were the generation who defined "rebellion." How could it happen between us, our kids, that distance…

I'm not talking about the span of miles between New York and Los Angeles. I'm referring to the distance across the kitchen table, the remoteness between two rooms in the same house.

The personal reserve that lack of effective communication can create gives the air around us a sense of infinite depth and incalculable fear of loss. We don't know how it came to be. Weren't the shared Sunday dinners and family movie night enough to create the strong bond of trust? How about the hug and kiss shared every morning—doesn't that create the environment where we and our child can share feelings, concerns, fears, and joys of the day?

Apparently, not always.

Life is changing around us so quickly; it's hard to figure out what our role should be as parents. The rules of conduct are bending and we can't quite find the right instruments to straighten out the situation. So, what is bending, changing shape, and making communication with our children so difficult? We are.

In today's world, it is getting harder than ever to show fear or weakness to our children. If we give in to despair, we might unravel the tenuous strings holding the family together. Emotionally, many of us can't let that happen. We may feel compelled to show a strong face turned toward the storm and allow it to pummel us unmercifully while we stand strong—even as we silently shout inside for someone else to take over the point position.

Women learn to isolate, evaluate and eliminate "messy" feelings of inadequacy, reserve, passion, intensity, sadness, or weariness. Ladies, I encourage you to simply put it on a shelf, and close the cabinet door—better yet, put a child lock in the handle. Make it difficult to retrieve those unpredictable emotions in a moment of weakness.

So the conversation begins with your child—

"How was school today?"

"Fine."

"Did anything interesting happen at school?"

"Just the usual stuff."

"Are you still dating that nice junior?"

"No."

"Why not?"

"It just didn't work out… just leave me alone!"

Flinching, we retreat hastily to the television, computer, or book muttering, "Wow. They must be having a bad night." We think it's better to leave them alone—just give them their "space."

I believe the only way to eliminate the distance between parents and children is to stride right over to the cabinet, dismantle the child lock and fling open the door. If rejection is the emotion you feel, yank it out and embrace it. Face your child with love and show them how you really feel. We don't need to be a martyr; just let them know the impact of their tone. If a child wants to hurt you, they can. It is how we handle it that shortens the distance between generations.

We have to be honest with ourselves and our loved ones if we ever want true trust, companionship, and a future. At the very least, we will know we have made an effort. Perhaps by example, those around us will raid the cabinet more frequently until it's empty.

Our child can't fully appreciate us as an individual until we cross the great divide. Begin your journey to dispel the distance. And don't look back.

■ What do you wish to have happen for your children?

Genuinely curious, I asked this question to discover what other mothers wished for their kids. Personally, my goal for our son consisted of having him reach adulthood with a good head on his shoulders and the common sense that God gives us all. I left the rest up to him. When asked, the women who answered my question proved we were of like mind and that pretty much proves to me that motherly love is universal when it comes to the wishes we have for our children.

■ *Have a purpose that is greater than themselves; use their talents and be true to their nature.*

Have any of you have been terrified that your children would want to make a living at an unexpected talent they displayed? Let's get real, not all skills are right for human observation or consumption! Watching the reality show America's Got Talent this past season made me realize that all of these people have parents! For example, one man's talent was surviving body piercings and sticking long bands of iron up and through his nose. Another hung hooks and swung bricks attached with chains from his eyelids. Can you image the mother that walked in and saw their children experimenting with that talent? I'm betting a neighbor called 911 as she screamed bloody murder.

The wish for a child to look beyond their own "me" and observe the world around them is vital. If it wasn't for the contributions and dedication of a select few, many opportunities may never have surfaced for those less fortunate. We know as we age, what we get comes from what we give.

■ *Live with no regrets.*

Someone asked my husband what he would do differently in his life. Rick beamed at the question, then me, as he said, "Nothing." Considering he had been married to me since the national centennial, that statement melted my heart.

I, however, can't say the same thing. Life throws curveballs when you least expect it. I'm amazed that I survived with all my limbs intact:

¤ I peeled the ivory keys off my mother's new baby Grand piano at the age of six and used permanent magic marker to make the ivory keys into a deck of playing cards. Amazed that I'm still breathing.

¤ I went on an afternoon date with a boyfriend to an archery range. Having no experience in the sport, he made an effort to show off his prowess by taking the stance of a warrior, lifting the bow and shooting an arrow straight up in the air. Horrified, I stepped toward him to stop him. He hadn't considered that the arrow had to return to earth and that trajectory would bring it right back to us. I still feel the rush of air and hear the "thump" of the returning arrow as it landed in the exact spot I had just left. That was our last date.

¤ I'm still trying to resolve my feelings about my brilliant best friend, Julie, who became pregnant at sixteen and left school. This was my first under-standing of the implications of sex. Keeping the baby, her life changed forever because the taboo of teen pregnancy still existed in the 70's. As I look at the world now through mature eyes, I realize I could have been a better friend, but I didn't know how.

I made a choice over thirty years ago to focus on what is right with the world and to trust my instincts explicitly. When I met my husband, Rick, for the first time, I knew then we would be married. On our second date, I advised him not to return unless he planned on marrying me; his expression—priceless.

He showed up on my doorstep three days later and I asked,

"You know what this means, right?"

"Yup," he replied.

"Why did you come back?" I inquired.

"This is too interesting not to see where it leads..." He smiled and shrugged.

Over thirty years later, he is still my best friend and personal savior. It doesn't get better than that.

- *Purchase good insurance.*

  Isn't it just like a mother to concentrate on the practical! I didn't have a lot of information growing up, so it resulted in me learning from my experiences with no sage advice. For example:

  - Too terrified of the entire pregnancy process, I had the bliss of ignorance. As a newlywed, my farmer husband escorted me to the pig barn to observe the birth of piglets. At first, mesmerized, I felt relief when it appeared so easy for the sow. Horrified shrieks erupted from my mouth when the mother lunged forward to try and eat one of her new-born babies. Reaching into the pen, I snatched it from the mother and clutched it to my chest. I wondered for weeks whether human mothers eat their young and how did the media cover it up?

  - My mother assured me that there is no such thing as an ugly baby. I wept when our son Ben nestled in my arms shortly after delivery. I wasn't relieved that the ordeal was over nor was I expressing tears of joy to finally be meeting our child for the first time. I cried because my son was a cone head like the aliens depicted on an old Saturday Night Live television show. When I saw Ben's head, malformed due to the birth process, all I could think of was he would have to wear a tall stocking hat for the rest of his life. Two physicians tried to convince me that his head would round out and he would look wonderful within two weeks. I bought a stocking cap anyway.

¤ Cookie sheets should have a warning label. Vigorously wiping off a metal cookie sheet with a cotton towel, I applied a bit too much pressure. My husband said something behind my back, and distracted me. My dishtowel and right hand flew off the top of the cookie sheet. A resounding "WHAP" filled the kitchen as the metal sheet bounced back to hit me in the face. My husband's only comment "Good thing it wasn't the frying pan."

¤ I needed to clear twelve inches of drifted snow out of our driveway while my husband worked out of town. Since this is a designated "man's job" in our household, I had never used the equipment. I pushed the heavy-duty snow blower out onto the drive. Buffeted by high winds, I staggered as I turned the key, pushed any button I could find and yanked the power cord; after five times it finally came to life. For the next two hours, I used every muscle I had to shove and pull the blower up and down the driveway and sidewalk.

That evening I declared my success to Rick regarding how it only took me two hours to complete. He sighed and gently wondered why it took two hours to do a twenty minute job. Then he asked, "Did you engage the self-propelling feature of the snow blower?"

¤ My mother made sure that I knew how to create the perfect meatloaf by watching her and copying her actions. She'd place the molded meat into the oven, light a cigarette and play single-handed bridge games in the dining room. She became so immersed in her game, she'd often forget to turn the temperature back from 425 to the 350 degree mark. Meatloaf would come out with a hard crispy exterior; with plenty of ketchup it actually grew on me.

I prepared our first married meal utilizing our family recipe of meatloaf, baked it at 425 degrees for three hours, put out a full bottle of ketchup and placed a sharp steak knife by our plates. Staring at me with a look of utter disbelief, he watched me attack the meatloaf with hacking blows. Rick took over cooking all of our meals and I haven't sawed through a meal since.

What I've never really gotten over, though, are the following two comments. No parent ever wants to survive their children, as these two women so poignantly express:

- *That they would have lived… I lost my youngest daughter, Samantha, twenty-eight years old and her two children, my grandchildren Caitlyn age six, Carter age two. Their house caught fire and blocked her escape. Her husband worked the late shift and was not there. She could not get out without her children so she got them into a place to wait it out. I am sure she was praying and hoping the firemen got there fast. But they didn't. The heat was intolerable. I watched this happen because they lived right behind me. A lot of me died with them. They were all placed in one coffin because you are not so big when you are a baby. They were not burned—they died from smoke inhalation. I did get to kiss my beautiful baby's cheeks and rub her body that early morning in October, 2005.*

- *That my daughter would have lived past thirty-three years.*

As I read those two comments, I cried, and all I could think of was that the best thing our children could ever possibly teach us is that we need to love them, to show them that love, and to tell them frequently because you never know when it will be all stripped away.

Above all, though, I go back to my own mother and what I hope my mother wanted for me. It wasn't always easy to figure out. A feminist, before the world applied the word to career-minded women, my mother had been born a generation too soon. A college education and being self-sufficient continually surfaced in her "life" discussions with me. Yet, contradicting herself, she would often extol the virtues of finding the right man and being a good wife to him. Regardless of her push to rear me as a fearless woman, I often witnessed her idolizing men and deferring to the masculine opinion over a women's recommendation most of the time.

What, exactly, is the message I'm supposed to learn as her daughter? It's alright to be smart, competent and build a career for myself, but none of that matters if it is different from what my spouse thinks? It took years trying to figure that one out.

We raised our son to respect and honor women and encouraged him to marry a woman who would make him a better man. In June 2009, we witnessed our son's marriage to his wife, Ashley. The caring way he watches out for her warms our hearts. They are in the union for the long run and we can't wait to see what life holds for them.

Let's learn from the advice of these women and then:

1. Take ownership of the way we communicate with our children.

2. Be brave in revealing our feelings and find a way to connect with trust and respect.

3. Don't think any incident or learning experience is too trivial. You never know when you might prevent someone from knocking themselves out with a frying pan.

We've survived the hard knocks and hope our children pay attention well enough not to experience the stress like we did. It's the best we can do.

Chapter Fifteen

The Benefit of Hindsight

G etting straightforward advice without any strings attached seemed like the perfect way to end this survey of self-reflection.

Perspective is worth its weight in gold. The experiences incurred during our lifetimes taint our ability to react to new information or interpret the meaning behind current circumstances. Sometimes, *not* making a judgment is extremely hard to do because our emotions and reactions are developed over time and become embedded as an essential element of who we are.

During lunch in a crowded restaurant, I overhead a man tersely state to the weeping woman across the table, "You knew what I was before you married me." I did a double take. Are we only a collection of our past experiences and therefore doomed to repeat behaviors? I prefer to believe that with insight into our emotions, we can work diligently to redefine the path of our lives.

■ What are the top life lessons women would benefit from knowing?

Here is your opportunity to evaluate the life lessons these women have shared with you. Some will make you sigh, others will generate a chuckle. Perhaps purpose and strength can be gleaned from these responses and will help you overcome whatever current issues you face. The following is the advice

I've chosen to highlight as these comments really hit home for me in recognition of the simple truth:

- *Don't be a martyr for your children; it weakens your self-worth.*

- *The man you marry may be your Prince Charming; however he may not have the prince's bank account.*

- *Don't be afraid of being alone.*

- *You can't please everyone.*

- *Embrace change without whining.*

- *Stay close to your girlfriends; men often come and go, parents die, we don't all have sisters that are so like us, we would choose them as friends; your girlfriends can last a lifetime and often do, and they will be there when no one else will.*

- *Surround yourself with people smarter than you are.*

- *The answer is always no, if you don't ask!*

- *Life is a banquet—don't starve!*

- *Not making a decision to do something is a decision itself.*

- *If a man is spending most of the time looking at your boobs during a conversation, he is really not worth it.*

- *When you are a size eight, you are not fat! Now that I'm a size sixteen, I wish I would have spent more time enjoying when I was a size eight.*

- *You have to learn to control your attitude or it will control you.*

- *Someone else can always do your job, no one is irreplaceable.*

- *It is often rare that one can choose how they die, but you can certainly choose how you live.*

- *You are not your past; you can create your future.*

- *Treat people nice, but don't get stepped on.*

- *Smile—it's the cheapest thing you have that you can give others.*

- *Stop comparing yourself to others, compete against yourself, be better today than you were yesterday.*

It takes courage to fully experience being a woman and a lot of this advice is about facing up to practical truths. Growing up, my primary resource for understanding the concept of courage was the movie, *Wizard of Oz*, watching the odd foursome face peril after peril. Confront the Wicked Witch of the West? No way. The Cowardly Lion with clanking knees, shaking shoulders, and quivery voice cowered in a corner hoping he might pass being noticed.

But then he did a strange thing. Despite his overwhelming fear, he faced the Wizard, spoke up to the Witch and battled flying monkeys. Why did he do that? If he had just walked in a different direction or bowed his head appropriately, he could have gone on with his life as the overlooked, insignificant being he wished to be. Instead, he stuck his neck out. So why did they call him the Cowardly Lion when in fact he never was? (That *was* the whole point of the movie!)

I think as women, we are like that. The true strength of our conviction and ability isn't often recognized immediately. What may appear to be submissive behavior may be in reality a way to bide our time until it is right to act. Often, we stand in awe of celebrities, managers, and public officials. Their glamour, authority, uniforms, and absolute control can make them icons in our perspective. Some of us never lose this automatic tentativeness around authority.

For example, let's say you receive a letter with an attorney's name and address on the envelope. The first reaction may be "what did I do?" Your hands might actually sweat as you slice open the envelope. Then a burst of laughter erupts when you realize it is only a solicitation for a local charity event. Your thundering heart slows and you can actually hear again because the blood that rushed to your ears has receded.

This adrenaline rush, shortness of breath, blushing ears, and copious sweating are all signs of how we react to authority figures. Yet, the attorney is just another human being working for a cause bigger than himself. His title is what he does, but his title is not what he is.

Now that women are a common sight in the workforce, we are learning to cope with the inadvertent power associated with our careers. I've learned that I affect others without even knowing it. I'm a mother, served as a Regional Manager, have held a Board position for a national association, and have served as a community Chamber of Commerce Chairperson. Others treated me respectfully, and some actually experienced anxiety when they spoke with me.

But…it's just me!

Once the mantle of authority is placed on our shoulders, the assumption of power over other's lives settles in. It not only takes courage to stand firm in front of an authority figure, but our own outward display of courage is absolutely critical. However, we can't be something we are not. People will know that we are faking it and then our credibility plummets.

What does this all have to do with advice for and by women? Simple. We are passing our knowledge on to help smooth out the path for others—call it a long-distance type of mentoring.

To this day, the Cowardly Lion remains an icon for me, reminding me that our own acts of courage create the texture of our existence through words, acts, and decisions.

This advice is a way of sharing possibilities and building faith that our collective strength can change the world. Think about what women have accomplished over the years:

- Rosa Parks refused to sit at the back of the bus, altering race relations nationally.

- Norma Rae blew the whistle.

- Margaret Thatcher governed England with a strong hand.

- A teenage girl births a child and gives it up for adoption.

- Mothers send their children off to school for the first time.

- Three-hundred-pound woman has a gastric bypass and loses 150 pounds.

- One-hundred-twenty-five days without an alcoholic drink and the woman smiles...

- A man and woman say, "I Do!" and mean, "Until death do us part..."

- Dying, my mother in hospice says, "That's enough," and says goodbye to those she loves.

Chapter Sixteen

My Own Straight Talk

Have you ever finished a project only to smack your forehead and say, "Dang it. I forgot to do that part?" Well, that's about where I am now. As I read through all my respondent's answers, as I collated them and started commenting on them, I realized that I left out two very important topics—one is a total "duh, Karel," for it deals with the issue of beauty, something no girl is immune to, and the other came to me in part because I kept seeing an underlying theme through everything my respondents wrote—and that is the issue of personal dignity.

So if it's okay with you, I want to go off on a couple of straight-talk rants here. Then look at those two areas, and as you read, I hope you'll see why I've put them here.

Beyond Beauty

I have to admit that I'm ecstatic the media is recognizing people are more than the package they are trapped in; that internal beauty is a vital element of a person's make-up. Take the following examples:

- ¤ The television series, *Ugly Betty*, bravely addressed the concept that beauty begins with personal integrity. The main character is ridiculed for obviously failing in fulfilling the beauty ideal. But despite everyone else's arrogance, this "average" person begins to shine. Betty is not only a survivor, she is

¤ an eternal optimist, believes in her intelligence, and demands respect which in turn generates awe.

¤ Dove Soap's advertising campaign depict women who more accurately reflect ageless feminine attributes: vibrancy, confidence, shapeliness, and pride in what they have to offer the world besides a perfectly balanced face. Are we finally beginning to look below the surface in order to discover the gems inside us?

Because it is human nature to make a judgment about another person within the first few seconds of meeting, we know the exterior needs to be maintained and that our individual expression of personality is enhanced by the way we dress. But, if we aren't governed by common sense and taste guidelines, we must be prepared to be evaluated and found wanting.

Do I always dress perfectly? Not on your life! In fact, often my husband shudders at the combination of tops and slacks I manage to throw together. Thankfully, he places a kind hand on my shoulder and urges me back to the closet to make a better choice.

Bless that man.

The current national health crisis focuses on the issue of weight. Reports in leading magazines and headline-stories on television lament the overweight issue for Americans. It's the clothing choices, however, that baffle me. I just don't understand the lure of wearing shirts and pants that are obviously two or more sizes too small. Every cellulite dimple, side roll, and goose bump patterns the garment like a relief map. At this state in life, I've been on this earth long enough to feel comfortable with the whole body-change thing. Yet, I know I must improve my physical condition by losing weight and exercising.

I wish there were drive-by cosmetic and medical facilities dedicated to transforming consumers at a reasonable price in an impressively short time frame. No suffering for nine months to starve off one pound a week, sweating on a treadmill, and instant-vision correction that eliminates the trifocals which are imbedded upon my nose.

We have mapped the human DNA for God's sake. When will someone figure out a way to keep skin firmly elastic like control-top panty hose? Or invent a pill that allows us to eat what we want and still maintain control of our bodily functions—you know—replace those weight loss tablets which transform the sugar and fat we ingest into a rumbling volcano. No, what we get is Botox which paralyzes a portion of skin around the injection site in order to smooth out wrinkles. That perpetually surprised expression is just so "in" this year!

Maintenance of our bodies is a good thing, but not to the exclusion of building a better "us" as we age. We also need to reinforce what we value…close confidantes, loving children, a secure financial situation and a purpose in life. Our perspective has to expand to move from judging only by the external and looking inward—to appreciating the beauty in everything around us.

We make decisions and choices every day, every hour, every minute regarding our looks and physical health. Why not pick the option that will bring you closer to your ideal self? I encourage you to not let others sidetrack you from your objective. Concentrate, be firm, and choose wisely. Then, don't regret the decisions you make.

Take a personal pledge to concentrate on building a healthy body, affirming life with your family and loved ones, and celebrate the fact that you exist at all in this dynamic world. Let's take creative license and change the chant reverently uttered in the comedy segment from *Saturday Night Lives'* "Wayne's World," and shout out, "We Are Worthy! We Are Worthy!"

It's about Dignity

I have no idea how people endure public judgment by appearing in a reality television program.

Who knew that thousands of individuals would line up in the street, swamp network e-mail systems or cram into arenas just for the chance to appear on a national television show, regardless of the subject matter? I'm distressed by the willingness of these participants to give up their dignity in return for the hope of winning a monetary prize. Ultimately, I believe the desire for celebrity appears to be the most compelling reason to enter into these situations.

Consider the program called *Super Nanny.* Granted this child expert has some really potent and vital information to share with overwrought parents, but why would anyone want to expose the dysfunctional aspects of their family for the entire world to view or show people how you can't manage the temper tantrum of a two-year-old child or disrespectful attitude of a pre-teen thug? When did it become fashionable to show the world how ineffective we really are? Recently a family in my local area was highlighted on the program and the local newspaper made sure everyone knew the time of the program and identified the family. I wonder how they react in the grocery store when they are recognized—proud because they got on a national television show or embarrassed because they couldn't control the program editing process?

Wife Swap found families that were willing to exchange wives for a two week period. Producers set it up so that diametrically different lifestyles and moral values clashed for the amusement of the audience. I just can't help thinking that this is a prelude to the sexual adult version called a key party—where couples gather for cocktails, put their keys in a bowl, and then leave for the night with another partner by digging into the bowl and drawing out a key chain at random. *Ewwwww.*

But let's look a bit closer… why didn't they name it *Husband Swap*? I was more disgusted at the revival of the concept that women are no more than chattel or personal property of the husband to be exchanged at will. By accepting the programming, aren't we, as females, supporting the concept and acting in our own worst interest?

Not a strong enough argument for you? Then let's examine *The Bachelor* where twenty gorgeous women are housed in a property—sounds like a harem to me. The look of the male analyzing the gathered herd of ladies makes me cringe. There hasn't been a woman on that program who could be remotely considered "average." Each is extremely beautiful, yet they participate in this cattle call. And to top it off, when they aren't selected, the whole world knows they've been rejected; that's got to be worse than being an overly tall or overweight eager girl standing along the wall hoping someone will ask her to dance. At least, as the wall flower, they aren't in the spotlight and if things don't go well; they can duck out the door, no one the wiser. The public humiliation of women maneuvering to be "picked" by the man just makes me sad.

Don't even get me started on evaluating the motives of individuals who appear on shows like *Jerry Springer* or *Maury Povich*. I recently watched a program where DNA results were revealed on air to prove or disprove a man was the father of a woman's child. The interpersonal exchange between previous romantic partners ranges from hysterical to pure brutish behavior. The audience urges them on with screams of pure delight. I feel it is reminiscent of the ancient Coliseum in Rome where the masses could watch as people died for their entertainment.

To me, voyeurism means living through the eyes of others. Do we watch reality shows in order to not think about what is happening in our own lives or gain perspective that "at least it isn't as bad as…"? I worry about the children who are subjects of reality shows or subjected to paparazzi because of their parent's celebrity status or those individuals brutally exploited when they display absolutely no talent and are held up for public ridicule.

Reality programming isn't only about the outrageous or dysfunctional; it includes showcasing personal perseverance as well. Programming dedicated to allowing the masses to have a chance to show off their unique talent is compelling; *American Idol, So You Think You Can Dance, America's Got Talent* are all examples of public auditions that draw thousands of participants. The range of artistic ability is staggering and the emotional drama compelling.

Of course, program editors relish in exposing the purely absurd act, such as a woman whose single talent was fitting into a suitcase. How she even thought that could carry an hour long Las Vegas show is beyond me. However, when an unexpected jewel steps out onto the stage, the viewing public collectively becomes emotionally involved.

The world loves a fighter, but when it comes down to women… we may need to rethink that. As women, we not only work hard to make the world an easier place in which to live, but we also want to be able to show our "backbone" and not be labeled with a tasteless derogatory term. We understand that society influences us from an early age. Whether we are naughty or nice may very well depend upon whose point of view we are referencing. Our humor, sense of right and wrong, and basic personality are molded into an acceptable shape, fitting nicely with the cultural scheme of things.

Society is comprised of human prototypes of all sizes, shapes, and intelligence. As an efficient society, we love to place labels on personality types: poised, civic minded, snobbish, plastic, robust, rowdy, cute, ugly, creepy, dangerous, a lost cause. The list grows as we age, having established our own criteria for each category. Labels help us orient ourselves and determine the manner in which we interact with a specific type of personality. "Keep things safe," ensures our perspective is sound.

By utilizing labels to categorize people, we may fail to see what is not readily evident—a treasure trove just waiting for exploration. The greatest tragedy is the knowledge of others we might have learned yet threw away because we reacted to first impressions.

Sitting quietly in a hotel bar enjoying my late night meal, a Karaoke session started. I looked up to watch the first person sing. Standing hesitantly in front of thirty people in the bar, an overweight woman stared down at her feet. I could hear the snickers of laughter and snide comments about her appearance. Limp brown hair whispered across slumped shoulders as the stage lights glared off her sweating forehead. Her dress was shapeless and worn—completely unflattering to her generous figure. Still she waited patiently for the technician to begin her song. Jeering persisted from her well dressed female co-workers as they urged her onward. Their faces registered the expectation that they would witness a delightful scene of embarrassment that they could gossip about at the office the next day. I wondered whether the singer's desire for companionship was so great that she would take the sneers in order to win their approval.

Expecting a train wreck performance, I listened as the music streamed from the loudspeakers with the opening notes for "The Rose," by Bette Midler. And then, beauty entered the room.

The lone singer's voice softly explored the corners of the bar, emotional and true. A tremulous beginning transformed into elegance and richness of sound, the room went mute; incredulous looks evident on many faces.

Singing with purity and soulfulness, my heart ached with the understanding that she sang this song for herself, not to entertain the enthusiastic crowd. As the music died away, the glow of exceptional talent dimmed. She stepped off the stage. Once again the meek, subdued woman, oblivious to the surge of excited applause and chants for "More!" left the room as she shook her head.

That night, I rediscovered that every person possesses a niche in life and a purpose to fulfill. What are your talents and desires? The manner in which you discover these essential elements about others is entirely up to you. It's about recognizing the power of human dignity and cherishing individual differences.

Chapter Seventeen

Essential Truths

You know, as I've thought about all these responses, it seems to me that so much of what we can learn from each other is personal responsibility. We have an enormous amount of strength, courage, and tenacity. We have had amazing mothers, fathers, and mentors who have helped shape who we are and how we see the world. But really, what it all comes down to is this, our actions have consequences and we are responsible for those consequences. Like most people, I learned this the hard way, and to show you what I mean, I would like to tell you a story.

One moment I'm playing softball with a highly skilled team of women on a ninety-five degree sunny day, the next I'm lying in a hospital bed. My body refused to respond to mental commands and the left side of my face appeared to have melted, drooping toward my shoulder. Unable to connect my thoughts enough to speak, the few words that did escape sounded like slurred soft mumbles. Vertigo and nausea a constant companion, I had trouble navigating the eating process.

Strangely enough, I had no concern at all about my condition. My gaze took in the soulful and scared expression of my husband, Rick, while he comforted our six-month old son near the side of my bed. My heart felt heavy with unbelievable regret; images of all the times I hadn't told Rick I loved him, how I fumbled with motherly duties, and the absence of our own family traditions.

Thoughts of extreme disappointment at the lack of a meaningful relationship with my parents dominated my conscious hours. As far as I knew, at the age of twenty-five, I would be wheelchair-bound unable to feed myself or hold a conversation again. And yet, regret weighed more heavily on me than thoughts about what I wouldn't be able to do in the future.

Suddenly the hospital privacy curtain whipped to the side and a cherubic face peered at the three of us. An older heavy woman with frizzy gray hair, moon-shaped face, wearing a gray volunteer uniform, leaned toward my husband and stated, "What? Tragedy? No time for that! I know exactly what you need!" She twirled around, her white orthopedic shoes squeaking on the linoleum, and reached into a metal cart positioned in the doorway.

With unbelievable adeptness, she returned to the bedside and shoved a *Sports Illustrated* magazine in Rick's unoccupied hand and announced, "No time to wallow in sadness. Read! Read and rejoin what is happening in the world!" Even though my face couldn't register my emotions, I laughed so hard internally I thought I might cut off my air supply. I know my eyes sparkled with delight at seeing the expression on Rick's face and our son Ben's fascination with this wild woman.

Almost as if she heard me, her head swiveled toward me and understanding showed in her ruddy features. The volunteer whisked out a Baby Ruth candy bar from her front pocket and tore off the top half of the wrapper. With a quick smile, she bent forward and shoved the candy into my half opened mouth, lodging it securely against my teeth. She held my chin and said "Everything is better with candy! Sweetness in your life...nothing like it!" My husband's abrupt laugh at the sight is something I remember to this day for the sheer joy of the sound.

The gray lady raised her hands chest high, palms outward and said softy, with unparalleled love, "There is always hope and possibility. Get on with life." Winking, she spun around, grabbed the cart handle and moved quickly around the corner into the hospital corridor.

I looked back at my husband only to see him shaking his head and watched a broad, knowing smile spread on his lips. Rick exclaimed loudly, "We can't even do this hospital scene right! We had the perfect soap opera and look what happens!" He tossed his head back and laughed loudly and fully.

It is my belief that our guardian angel visited us that day. In what seemed our darkest moment, her ray of hope gave Rick the strength to deal with a newborn baby and a potentially crippled wife, while it gave me a true chance for personal happiness and emotional calm.

At that moment, I knew that what I did in the future had nothing to do with my past. I could write my life story any way I wanted. Unable to express verbally these thoughts to those who loved me most, I realized I had to prepare to do battle within myself to solve the issues, real and imagined.

The clinical diagnosis began as Multiple Sclerosis, then we learned that medications used to treat MS created stroke-like symptoms for me. Once they discontinued the prescribed drugs, I began to get better. My face returned to the proper symmetry and the numbness in my left side began to fade. I finally held my son without supervision after twelve weeks; a milestone of such magnitude that nothing compares. Years later, Mayo Clinic ruled out the original diagnosis and determined that issues related to my childhood deadly bout with measles had damaged a few nerves in the brain and prescribed a medical regimen that gave me my life back.

In those months of silence, trapped in a body that wouldn't cooperate, I waged an internal war that not only made me stronger but allowed me to recognize an essential truth in life: that regret is a powerful emotional detriment. The wealth of information shared by the women who responded to the survey proves that connecting and sharing can provide insight that is invaluable, even if we may have been exposed to the concepts before. My mother's effort at raising me may have included conflicting messages, but I learned that life is messy. Sometimes we get it right on the first try and other times we struggle, never quite making contact when it counts the most. At least she tried to pass on her wisdom.

In order to keep focused about my own personal responsibility, I've developed a reality checklist in terms of essential truths. It's what keeps me honest, and it is the list by which I guide my life. I want to share it with you because it took a dramatic event before I finally understood how precious life was. I hit a brick wall rather than hitting my stride. In this book, I hope through collective insight we can skirt around the obstacles and anticipate change while welcoming with open arms whatever comes into our lives.

Information turned into wisdom has incredible healing power. Perhaps some of these truths will hit home for you and others may be your wake-up call. Fully planning on expanding this checklist with continued feedback from women I meet nationwide, I ask that you consider your own personal truth. Know that whatever it is, it's worth adding to the chorus of female voices as we announce to the world in the words of Helen Reddy, "We are women…hear us roar!"

■ Reality Checklist of Ten Essential Truths

1. You are not the center of the universe but part of a greater collective humanity. What hurts others ultimately harms you.

2. Your actions and words impact others. Try to take complete responsibility for how you interact with people and the decisions you make. Once that happens, I believe we are set free to live an unhampered life.

3. You are not inconsequential; you matter to yourself and to those who truly love you for who you are. With that strength of personal commitment, you show your children the path to their own strength.

4. The past can't be changed. You are a brand new person each day that you wake up. The experiences for the current moment mold you so you can face the challenges of the next day. Everything that happens to you has a purpose. It's up to you to learn the lesson and move on.

5. Create opportunity by the attitude you wear.

6. Earn the right to be part of someone's life. Don't suffer entitlement attitudes. Provide good and fair exchanges of personal value and then hope that your offering is recognized and access to friendship is returned. In the converse, people need to earn the right to be part of your life. There are throngs of individuals who shine in their love of others and ethical beliefs. It makes great sense not to make room for harmful, toxic people in your life, ever.

7. Refuse to be a victim of circumstance or any career situation. Set your path by the decisions you make and the personal ethics you hold. Don't fear vicious personalities; try to discover what made them that way

and gain an understanding for what motivates them. Acknowledge the behavior and move on.

8. Seek perspective and work continually not to be wounded by toxic people who take joy in dishing out cruelties. Looking for the source of an attack may reveal a perceived slight, professional jealousy, or something that has absolutely nothing to do with you. Keeping a personal distance and not reacting before you fully understand the dimensions of the conflict can prove to be a wise course of action.

9. Don't apologize for your personal idiosyncrasies. Whistle softly while you shop, sing opera in the car, stop and make chattering noises at squirrels, or tear up at a movie trailer. If they are going to love you, they have to love all of you.

10. Let emotional calm rule when chaos surrounds you. When people are counting on you to have emotional balance, step back, observe, and react to accurate information. Then, after a highly charged event, get through the hyperventilation or tears in private. Just like the commercial says, "Never let them see you sweat."

I'm a fatalist and I believe things happen for a reason and that people enter our lives when we most need them, even if we don't understand why they are there. I've experienced intense connection with people for no obvious reason, but it eventually is revealed they either have something to teach me or I am there to help them.

Try to accept your personal journey for what it is: an opportunity to grow into the ultimate person you're supposed to be.

Acknowledgements

I'd like to thank all of the women who responded to the lengthy survey and provided me with this exceptional information to pass on. I'll do my best to make sure your message of hope, encouragement, and joy is experienced by as many people as possible. It's the least I can do to honor your time, insight and commitment to mentor other women.

And Mom, wherever you are…I was listening.

Appendix

Condensed Survey Results

To view the entire survey, go to www.HittingOurStride.net for the download.

Summarized Responses

As promised, here are the summarized responses to all the questions I asked my group of dedicated, strong, intelligent, and amazing women. Don't try to read them all at once. Instead, use this as a form of *tiramisu* which means "little-pick-me-up" in Italian. When you need inspiration, find a section that inspires you. When you need comfort…well, you get the idea.

I hope you enjoy them and learn from them as much as I did.

■ What is your greatest personal strength?

- Empathetic, care about people, emotional intelligence
- Dedication, determination, tenacity, perseverance, and commitment
- Positive personality, optimistic point of view
- Independent of thought, stand up for what I believe in, visionary
- Adaptable—get along with people, understand different points of view
- Religious faith and spirituality
- Driven to succeed
- Communication, persuasive, and effective
- Organization skills
- Lifelong learner
- Decision-maker and leader
- Resilient, belief in abilities

- Loyal and reliable
- Creative, problem solver
- Patient
- Trusted, common sense
- Honest
- Manage money well

■ What scares you the most?

Personal / Family

- Losing those you love
- Loneliness
- AIDS
- Being without my sight
- Getting old and not being able to take care of myself
- Failure
- Bad health

Children / Next Generation

- The difficulties my children will face. We live in such uncertain times.
- Our children, especially girls, think that it is normal to have sex immediately after they meet someone.
- What scares me the most is leaving my child in the world with so many unknowns.
- Prices are going up and wages are going down—it's a struggle to get by.

- The safety of my children in today's society.
- I do not think the children of today have enough empathy for others.
- Lack of purpose in youth.
- That my teenage son is "experiencing" the world and hasn't acquired all of the tools to deal with it yet.

Economy

- A declining economy
- National debt
- Political budgeting priorities and miss spending of tax dollars
- It scares me to see how a lot of people are taking our planet and each other for granted. It also scares me to see how bad the economy is now and what ramifications it is going to have when my children are grown ups.

Government / Society

- War (nuclear or biological)
- Inept politicians
- Too much power in too few hands—government too much in control
- Lack of effective leadership in government
- Big Brother—history does not bode well on this
- Incarceration without lawyers or charges being filed; I cannot imagine what I would do if I was the one picked up or if one of my children "disappeared." I wish I could say I trust that it is used only in extreme circumstances; suspicion is not always correct.

- War on American soil
- We seem to get caught up in things that really don't matter and those things become the drivers of our society—ignoring the issues.
- Changing dynamics in the world strength—political uncertainty
- Negative world view of our nation
- The shift of wealth to the hands of a few
- The condition of our infrastructure and the lack of funding to fix it
- Lack of privacy pertaining to our social security number and personal records kept
- Lack of good health care for all
- Immigration
- Current presidential choices
- People that are running things all over the world just don't seem to understand that this is it; there is no other place to go to and we are not working together to defeat hunger and sickness yet we spend billions to try and kill each other.
- Our enemies

Religion

- Religious zealots / fanatics
- Religious hatred, genocide
- The battles over religious beliefs
- My loved ones will not know about salvation
- Pure evil

- Living without the growing knowledge of the Lord and his word

Finances

- Financial challenges; not being financially secure
- Rising costs

Violence

- Terrorism
- Violence against children and others
- Lack of regard for a human life
- Drug abuse
- Crime, school shootings
- Violence on the news, especially when directed toward infants and kids
- All the scary people—people on drugs and sociopaths
- Fear of the general population

Environment

- Environmental issues
- Diminishing resources
- Extinction without conscience
- Irresponsibility for our actions to others and our environment
- Bad weather

Culture

- Lack of values or morals of the nation and younger generation

- Fracture of the nuclear family
- Apathy, closed minds, complacency
- Lack of appreciation and respect for the law and others
- Entitlement and selfishness attitude
- The overwhelming need of the younger generation for instant gratification…a sense of "entitlement" with waiting, working, earning, deserving
- No accountability for actions
- All the hate in the world
- Ignorance
- Lack of women's self-esteem
- Lack of face-to-face communication—impersonal electronic communication
- That no one will stand to make a difference
- Lack of shame, responsibility
- Not learning from history what does or does not work
- The pace of the world is too fast. No one feels like they can keep up. Yet, they are afraid to get off. The time is flying by very fast.
- Lack of loyalty from people, organizations, even families
- All the damaged brains from drug abuse
- Lack of self-control
- Racism
- Escalating acceptance of bad manners, poor taste, all being seen by our children

- Over-population/over-dependence on fossil fuels—
loss of individuality as the world becomes smaller and
smaller

- It seems like America is always wanting the "status"
of "we can do it all" and places focus on countries that
need "help." We have so many people here that need
our help.

- Americans killing themselves with bad food choices
and no exercise

- That we have forgotten the Golden Rule

- That no one knows how to survive when we do not
have all the luxuries

- The push to bottom (lowest denominator) by corporations and government

Technology

- Technology, streamlining everything

- The amount of information of personal information that is available on the Internet and the amount
information we are exposed to every day—good, not so
good, and downright terrifying

- That we've become so enamored of our technology that
we're too concerned with whether we can, not whether
we should

■ What is your greatest personal fear?

- Death of a family member or loved one as well as
dying, especially dying alone

- Personal illness and aging

- Being alone, unloved, rejected and unappreciated

- Out-living retirement funds that result in a lack of independence and winding up in a nursing home
- Fail to live up to my personal potential or be unable to truly experience life because of lack of money or time
- That our children will settle and not reach for more
- Unable to provide for children by being unemployed
- Unable to make a difference—having regrets about life choices because I played it too safe
- War, depression, holocaust, not able to keep children safe, loss of freedom
- Letting someone down
- Divorce or being a broken family / sharing custody of children
- Not having children or if I do, messing them up
- Traded in for another model
- Not going to heaven or losing faith
- Personal safety or a home invasion
- And then, if you thought you had it bad—Fear that life won't get any better than this…This year this is hard because I just lost a seven-month-old grandson, my office flooded with five feet of really awful water, I'm trying to help my eighty-five-plus-year-old mother and mother-in-law, my son's life is currently in chaos, and I have two sisters whose health won't let them live much longer.

■ How do you feel about the world we live in today using a few defining words?

Positive

- Fast paced, busy
- Exciting, hopeful, optimistic, incredible potential
- Big adventure—it is what you make it, opportunity
- Complex, diverse, challenging, choices
- Amazing, wonderful
- Information driven, intelligent, divisive
- Environmental responsibility, global
- Technology and medical opportunities
- Service and friendship oriented, connected, diversity
- Easy and safe place to live in, lucky to live in America
- Blessed, secure, free
- Good—living with purpose
- Community focus
- God is in control, prayerful
- Beauty

Negative

- Chaos, changing, evolving, unsettled, unlimited consequences, lack of balance, unpredictable
- Scary, dangerous, violent, war, heading for destruction, volatile
- Crazy, messed up, irresponsible, no commitment
- Materialistic, greed, we want it now!

- Loss of respect for life and people, human rights
- All about me attitude, entitlement attitude, not giving to others
- Too technology focused, over connected, information overload
- Poverty, debt
- Corrupt, polluted, poor, power-hungry leaders
- Apathy, hopeless, lack of accountability
- Struggle, pain, dissatisfied, unhappy
- Impersonal, disconnected, don't know much outside the US
- Nosy, judgmental
- Declining moral base, filth on TV
- No social skills, dysfunctional
- Ignorant, confused
- Intimidating, aggressive
- Competitive
- Disillusioned, no pride
- Instant gratification
- Disposable mentality
- Addiction
- Over-populated
- Godlessness
- Losing traditions
- Co-dependent
- Too much hate

Observations

- Life is a bowl of cherries, sometimes you hit a few pits; other times it's sweet.
- We make a difference in our own way, the question is what kind of difference do you want to make?
- History repeats itself—wars, torture, rich, poor
- Ever-shrinking world with so much misunderstanding
- Lack of foresight by those in authority
- Always on standby, never at ease
- Lack of long-term commitment
- Expanding and contracting at the same time

■ What lessons did you learn from your mother?

Career

- It's okay for a woman to choose a non-traditional career.
- Follow your dreams.
- Question authority.
- Make a good first impression.
- Be different; don't go with the status quo.
- Okay to make mistakes…just learn from them.
- Attention to detail
- Build variety into your life.
- Don't retire too early.
- No job is beneath you.

- Take charge of your life and career.
- Plan for the future.
- Don't worry about the things you cannot change.
- Like Scarlett O'Hara's father, Mom taught me, though inadvertently, the value in owning land
- Finish the job right even if it's cleaning the toilet.

Self-Reliance / Self-Esteem—Stand up for Yourself

- NOT to continually cave in to a man's thoughts on what he wants you to be.
- Self-worth begins with a good self-image; don't let others walk all over you.
- Stand tall and be proud of yourself.
- Stand up for yourself and your beliefs.
- Never give up on yourself; believe in yourself.
- Be independent—don't rely on someone else to take care of you.
- Take charge and responsibility for your own life; don't be a victim.
- Do whatever it takes—you can do anything you put your mind to.
- Don't need a man to make you happy or whole.
- Don't live life based on a man's emotions of the day.
- Be honest and true to yourself—be your own person / love yourself.
- Don't let circumstances dictate who you are.
- Never restrain yourself, your children or others from their potential.

Success

- Work hard and think smart to accomplish daily goals.

- Multi-task—juggling family, work and sanity

- Evolve

- Keep learning, go to school and stay mentally active.

- Don't be a sucker.

- Know what you excel in; do what you love and support others who are doing the same because the money will follow.

- Appearances are important; look your best.

- Have a positive outlook; when one door closes, another opens.

- Volunteer

- Have fun every day.

- Don't take no for an answer—look for another way.

- Achieve your own dreams, not what others want for you.

- Be prepared.

- Pay attention to details.

- Follow the rules.

- Always leave a place better than you found it.

- When in doubt—don't.

- If you are going to do a job, do the job right.

- Be practical and efficient.

- Have common sense.

- Always try your best at all that you do.

Endurance

- Change happens, roll with the punches and be resilient.

- Respect your body—be as active as much as you can.

- Life isn't fair. Do the best you can with what you have because there is someone who is always worse off.

- Never give up; if bad things happen, get back up and keep moving forward, it'll turn around.

- Keep doing something until you get it right.

- Choose your battles.

- Be realistic.

- Make careful choices.

- Take care of yourself—no one else will.

- Don't cry in public, be tough.

- You can survive a physical and emotional breakdown.

- Sacrifice sometimes carries a big price.

Relationships / Family

- Treat others as you wish to be treated—Make them feel important.

- Find the good in everyone.

- Spending time with my family is more important than a clean house.

- Your family's welfare should come before your perceived happiness because blood is thicker than water.

- Life is too short to not say all the things you want to; if you wait too long they may be gone.

- Protect your family—always be there for them.

- Listen to your children. Raise independent, responsible children and let your children live their own life.
- Never choose a man over a friend.
- Never forget you were a couple first; you need to work at any kind of relationship to maintain them and have them flourish.
- Be kind when you can and firm when necessary.
- Make time for fun every day.
- Don't play favorites.
- Give others the benefit of the doubt—we don't know what they are struggling with.
- Judge people by their heart, not their weaknesses.
- Be a good friend.
- Don't judge others by appearance.
- Listen carefully to what others say; give them feedback and fully engage in every opportunity for one on one exchange.
- Consider how your actions affect others; actions have consequences.
- Do not make waves.
- Gossiping doesn't feel good to anyone.
- Your husband is head of the household.
- You don't owe your family.
- You can do too much for people.
- Forgiving others doesn't make them right, but it sets you free.
- A mother's priority full-time job/career is to take care of the home and family and her marriage.

- You cannot please everyone.
- Tomboys are not popular at prom time.

Relationship Communication

- Communication is the key to intimacy.
- Listen to their stories and share.
- To be outgoing and social
- You can never take back words, so watch what you say to someone.
- It doesn't hurt to hold your tongue sometimes.

Character

- Strength in adversity
- Persistence and perseverance
- Stoicism
- Love unconditionally.
- Be hospitable, considerate, nice and polite.
- Sense of humor—laugh
- Respectful of others and of yourself; value people for what they offer.
- Compassion
- Positive attitude
- Honesty
- Patience
- Never say "can't" or complain—Go for it.
- Kindness
- Humility

- Integrity
- Be giving and share
- Loyalty
- Determination and disciplined
- Finish what you start; don't be a quitter.
- Non-judgmental and fair
- A forgiving heart
- Treat everyone equally; stand up for those who can't stand up for themselves.
- Courtesy
- To show emotions is a sign of weakness.
- Unselfishness
- Presentability
- Grateful
- Creative
- Optimistic
- Accountable and responsible
- Strength
- No one likes a smart ass.

Finance

- Count change; always live under your income level, rather than above by not spending more than you make.
- Never be completely dependent on your spouse; depend on people but, stay independent.
- How to stretch a dollar

- Always have a separate bank account with some money in it.

- Give generously and be thankful that you have it to give.

- Pay your bills.

Spirituality

- Faith and reverence for God

- Never cease praying and always be thankful to God.

- Religious beliefs help people deal with difficulties; God is there to lean on.

- Govern all you do as if God was watching.

- We are powerful spiritual being, capable of creating anything we desire. We need to use that power wisely and ethically.

Practical

- Do not stare at people who have disabilities or your children may be born with the same thing.

- Keep a clean house.

- Choose to be happy—think good thoughts, appreciate what you have.

- Take care of yourself—without your health, nothing else matters.

- Things aren't always what they seem.

- Don't take a short cut across the neighbor's lawn (respect other people's property).

- How to shop; bargains are only bargains if you were going to buy that item anyway.

- Make your life an adventure, it is the only one you have.
- Worrying is a useless emotion—it gets you nowhere and does nothing for you.
- The best thing about telling the truth is you do not have to remember what you said.
- Use the good dishes, towels etc. on a regular basis!
- Don't wear holey undies out of the house.
- Life is not fair and people don't always act right.
- Don't go to bed in a dirty room.
- Learning to be patient will cause you less grief.
- Fold the clothes as you take them out of the dryer.
- Take a man with you to buy a car.
- Make sure you say, "Drive carefully," when someone leaves.
- Do not ever use the four letter word in this house. Ladies don't talk like that in public; always act like a lady.
- When one door closes another opens.
- Many hands make lighter work.
- If I was with friends that were getting in trouble, I would be the one to get caught.
- Pretty is as pretty does.
- Be sure to conduct yourself in public; people are watching.
- Savor every moment.
- That you can screw up and still be a good parent

- Not everything is as it seems.
- Good guys do not always finish last! If they do not pay your bills then do not worry about what they think of you.
- Nice little girls are to be seen and not heard.
- Use the common sense you were born with.
- Pack early.
- Life can be challenging but if you have a good sense of humor, things are a lot less serious!

■ What lessons did you learn from your father?

Self-Reliance/Self-Esteem—Stand up for Yourself

- The only one you can rely upon is yourself: believe that you can do whatever you choose. Commit to it and do it well.
- Speak your mind even if it isn't popular.
- What doesn't kill you makes you stronger—don't let the world eat you alive.
- To have courage, stay strong, but don't be afraid to let your weakness show.
- Be independent—buy real estate.
- I'm beautiful.
- Take risks; be brave and don't be afraid to get your hands dirty.
- Stick up for yourself because no one else will; you are worthy of respect.
- Never forget where you came from or your past.

- Gender roles are overrated—I can be better than any man.

- No one is any better than you are.

- Get a good education so you can be financially independent.

- Don't be afraid of failure or making a mistake.

- Walk quietly and carry a big stick.

- Not to require praise from someone else to know I have done well

- Don't let a man dictate your actions.

- Give a firm handshake and look people in the eye.

- The world doesn't owe you anything—you have to work for it.

- You'll always have what you need.

- If you're going to make that bed, you'd better be prepared to lay in it.

- Vote for yourself, you hate to lose by one vote.

- Always have a twenty dollar bill tucked away, just in case.

Success

- Work hard; you get what you work for.

- Education is important.

- Always do your best—take pride in your work because quality work is important.

- When something needs to be done, do it well—pay attention to details.

- Persistence and perseverance: finish what you start through discipline and commitment. Keep trying until you make something of yourself.

- Take chances—try something new.

- Be self-sufficient.

- Be on time.

- Keep your tools clean and organized.

- Sacrifice

- Set priorities and goals.

- Never show fear.

- Dream and have a vision for your future; embrace the power of positive thinking.

- Nothing is ever too late.

- Be respectful to those you serve and be loyal to them.

- Have passion and gusto; live life to the fullest.

- Be patient and deliberate; think things through because slow and steady wins the race.

- Servant leadership—lead by example.

- Keep your word—hold true to your commitments and obligations.

- Prepare for the worst; have two back up plans.

- Have a strong commitment to a cause—be active in civic engagement.

- Anything worth having in life is worth working for.

- You can always find work.

- Keep your ducks in a row, but it's okay if they get out of line sometimes since that happens in life.

- Always find the answers.
- Cultural differences are to be embraced and learned from.
- Everything is negotiable.
- Don't hold grudges.
- Stay out of trouble; everyone reads the police logs.
- The most valuable things in life are earned, not given to you.
- Use your mind not your hands to make a living.
- You're never above the consequences.
- Talk less, listen more.
- Trust your instincts (gut).
- Don't get involved in office politics.
- Don't use bad language.
- You are never too old to change.
- It's not always what you know, it is who you know.
- If you're going to get fired, get fired for doing your job.
- Look beyond the veneer in all things.
- Under promise and over deliver.
- Travel when you are healthy.

Endurance

- Life is short—live well with no regrets.
- Never give up. Endure with no complaints and if you fall, get back up.
- Tenacity and personal strength
- Hard work never killed anyone.

- You can do anything even in a man's world.
- Take time to smell the roses.
- Only we can change our own situations.
- If you want chocolate have chocolate.
- Be tough.
- Tomorrow is always a better day.
- Don't expect praise for everything you do.
- In an even race men win.
- Don't ever let anyone bring you down.
- Freedom is not free and to love our country

Relationships / Family

- Unconditional love by taking care of the family first
- Have fun and have a sense of humor; enjoy life.
- Embrace nature; learn to fish.
- Build great friendships and find time to help a person in need.
- Respect everyone regardless of their status in life and treat everyone honestly and fairly.
- Say "I love you" to the ones you love every day.
- Stay in touch with loved ones regularly.
- Don't judge people on appearances, but on what you know; accept them for who they are.
- Be kind and have compassion.
- Listen and think before you speak.
- Give back to others.
- Do things as a family and be fully present.

- Be a partner—marriage is a 'team' effort.
- You can't make everyone happy all of the time—learn to compromise.
- Loyalty
- Communication is the key to intimacy; never burn bridges.
- Enjoy sports.
- Be cooperative.
- Learn about other cultures.
- Men can cook and do housework too.
- Own up to errors and find a solution.
- Don't hurt anyone even if they hurt you; if you can't say something nice about someone, don't say anything at all.
- Praise the children.
- Earn respect.
- As long as you eat at my table and live under my roof you will be respectful of me.
- Ask your children what their goals are and what their tasks are now to realize that goal.
- Trust until someone gives you a reason not to; be careful who you trust.

Character

- Honesty
- Patience
- Enjoy life and the little things.
- Fairness
- Positive attitude

- Ethical
- Integrity
- Self-Depreciating
- Forgiveness
- Diplomacy
- A good citizen
- Understanding
- Responsible and trustworthy
- Always honor your word.
- Discreet
- Helpful
- Friendly
- Trustworthy
- Conservative
- Character is what you do when no one is watching.
- Gentleness is very manly.

Finance

- If you can't pay cash, you can't afford it.
- Always spend less money than you make—be frugal.
- Financial security and independence; budget and plan ahead financially by setting aside money for retirement.
- Money isn't the most important thing in life.
- You can always afford to save money.
- Set aside money for emergencies.

Spirituality

- Practice your faith.

- Believe in God and he will guide you through life—the good and bad times.

- Love God, family, and country, always.

Positive messages

- Count your blessings every day.

- Sometime silence is golden.

- Slow down. Always take time for a watermelon break and play because life is too short; fill your life with something positive.

- Take care of yourself.

- Tell it like it is.

- Keep your shoes shined and your shoe heels fixed.

- See the beauty of the world through the eyes of an artist.

- Left handers are the only ones in their right minds.

- Always keep a full tank of gas in the winter.

Negative messages

- Don't abandon the children.

- Critical and harsh words said to a child cannot be erased with an "I'm sorry."

- The world can be a very cruel place.

- No daughter of mine will ever take the place of a breadwinner.

- My father abused me; I learned not to hit people.

- Be temperate in food and drink; don't become an alcoholic.

- Most dads are pretty crappy.

- Do as I say and not as I do.

- People are no damned good.

- Not to believe much of what he said

- To not beat your spouse—my father was not a nice man.

- Sense of being less important than sons

- Men are selfish.

- It is a man's world.

- Not to trust men

- Hardness; I was brought up to work for food, clothes and shelter. When you "cried' to him, it fell on deaf ears because if you had the necessities, why worry and complain?

- Men deserve respect.

■ What did you learn about life by observing your parents?

- Work hard to get what you want—it pays off.

- Love is powerful—unconditional—and it can last.

- Importance and dedication to family and together time

- Spouses must work as a team—sacrifice for the children.

- Life isn't fair and no one said it would be—roll with the punches and support each other.

- Communicate positively—disagreements aren't permanent—deal with it and move on.

- That you don't have to have money to be "wealthy"

- Dedication—marriage is not easy but stick together even in the bad times.

- You can't make people do what you want them to do—work at the relationship.

- Everything can be worked through—life can be messy.

- Respect

- Stand up for yourself; you are the only person you can truly rely on in this life.

- Accountability; take responsibility for your actions and choices.

- Endurance; life requires strength and "hurts" don't have to destroy a relationship.

- Be positive; attitude does more to effect outcomes than situation itself.

- Love can be expressed beyond words.

- Opposites attract.

- Have outside interests.

- Be honest and do what you say you will do.

- Be conservative with your finances.

- Keep going forward—set goals.

- Make your own happiness.

- A loving family is a great "base of operations" for the rest of your life.

- Live life to the fullest.

- Be adaptable; solve problems with creativity, ingenuity, and faith.

- To be tolerant and enjoy the simple things in life; practice forgiveness.

- Faithfulness
- That the things in my life are replaceable
- Belief in God
- Don't settle—everyone deserves to be happy.
- The mother holds the family together…the daddy holds the mother's heart.
- Seeing that parents can also be best friends.
- Home should always be warm and comforting.
- A strong need for independence
- Be thoughtful of those less fortunate—it will reward you in your own life.
- Be willing to take risks if you want a better life.
- Be ambitious.
- Life is more enjoyable when you have someone to share it with.
- Don't take things for granted.
- Don't stay with someone who treats you badly or makes you miserable or stay married to your spouse because of your children.
- Things aren't always what they appear to be.
- Don't drink or fight.
- Parents have to be a united front and back each other up.
- It is tough to love people with mental illness.
- Volatile behavior causes others to walk away silently.
- Not everyone has a "huggy" family.

- Don't resent your parents for not being able to teach
  · something they simply did not know.

- Don't argue in front of your kids; unhappiness and resentment are poison to children.

- Time changes people.

- A woman will always have to fight and do better than a man and will still only get half the credit.

- Don't be a victim.

- Actions speak louder than words.

- Conflicts are hard to resolve when you aren't taught good resolution skills.

■ What does it take to build a strong, positive family that stays connected?

- Communication—keep issues out in the open.

- Unconditional love

- Shared experiences—meals, fun, reunions—quality time together

- Stay connected—dedication to each other

- Respect

- Faith

- Trust

- Understanding and empathy

- Active Listening and observation skills

- Honesty

- Independence; you can guide but not necessarily control.

- Learn to accept others for who they are.

- Forgiveness—people act as best they can at the moment given the circumstances.
- Teamwork and commitment
- Patience
- Parents that are role models and leaders
- Encouragement
- Dedication and loyalty
- Humor and fun
- Discipline and consistency
- Sharing and selflessness
- Compromise
- Don't hold grudges.
- Positive memories
- Compassion; be caring and considerate.
- Positive attitude
- Building each other up
- Perseverance and determination
- Strong values
- Kindness
- Fairness
- Traditions
- Acceptance
- Respect privacy
- Time
- Accountability for actions

- Live close
- Genuine interest in what other family members are doing
- Appreciation
- Be non-judgmental
- Never talk bad about your family to another family member.

■ What do you believe destroys the unity of a family?

- Lack of constructive communication
- Self-absorption; selfishness, greed, and indulgence that related to ego
- Deceit; lies and dishonesty that destroys trust
- Disengagement by parents and between family members
- Not physically spending time together due to a geographical disconnect
- Disrespect—secrets; gossip about other family members
- Alcohol (or other substance abuse)
- Negative emotions; bitterness, jealousy, anger
- Too busy and other outside influences
- Over control; manipulation and setting expectations by the parent for the child
- Infidelity; married with a singles lifestyle that results in a disposable relationship
- Lack of faith and a moral base

- Favoritism that results in unfair treatment
- Abuse; physical and mental (criticism, judgment, demeaning)
- No forgiveness
- Divorce
- Overlooking unacceptable behavior; not supporting accountable behavior.
- Money issues
- Competitiveness between family members; bickering and finding fault with each other
- Not listening and being fully present
- Immovable opinions; no compromise or understanding another point of view.
- Immature parents
- "Plugged in" rather than communicating face to face.
- Apathy and indifference
- Poor or no leadership by a parent—not teaching skills about relationships.
- Satan
- Immovable in opinions
- Parents being friends and not a parent
- Children left on their own
- Not being able to be yourself
- Bickering and finding fault with each other
- Absent parent and abandonment
- Denial
- Death

- Lack of insight—ignorance
- No traditions
- Pornography
- TV during supper
- Not living in the now; reverting or referring to long passed incidents or issues.
- Impulsiveness
- Letting outside influences effect attitude and decisions of the family more than the family unit itself.
- When siblings marry someone who the family disapproves of.

■ What is the hardest decision you ever had to make?

Marriage or Divorce

- Deciding to get married or not, then I realized that he was the first person I thought of in the morning and the first that I wanted to tell anything to.
- To stay in my marriage when things got rough
- Staying with my husband when I was about to 'have a breakdown' over his different views, based on his culture, on morality—there were several factors that played into my decision to finally leave. The first was my health from all of the anxiety. I was having heart palpitations and felt terrible and anxious all of the time. I don't know if this was because I had anxiety about the direction the relationship was heading, or my husband's on-line and physical "fooling around." The other HUGE factor for me was watching a colleague's husband pass away from cancer. They had not made it

to their first wedding anniversary. They were so in love and he was such a wonderful man. When I spoke with her about my situation she told me to not waste any time being unhappy or settling. Families rebuild and they are stronger when everyone is in a positive and healthy state.

- To fight to make my marriage work and to stay with my husband for our three sons who needed their father.

- I made the decision to leave an abusive husband because of the fear that my daughter would grow up without me.

- To get divorced knowing that brain damage had affected him, and he could be a potential danger to our children.

- To leave my marriage after twenty-seven years and six children by meeting someone who helped me find the courage.

- Divorce—I had to sit back and think of the ramifications of living with two children at a five dollar an hour job—talking with friends who knew what my husband had put me through for eighteen years. I would not have to be afraid anymore of being punched in the face or have a gun pulled on me. So many other horrid things he did to me…

- To go forward after my husband divorced me after twenty-five years—I had to accept the fact I needed to provide a roof over my head (and my two kids) and live on a budget as a school teacher.

- I had to decide to be both parents especially after my ex remarried immediately after our divorce was final.

- To leave my husband of nineteen years, knowing that I deserved a better, more loving life and having the support of my friends throughout it all.

- Divorce—realizing I could not subject myself and children to the abuse any longer.

- To get a divorce after twenty-nine years of marriage—I knew I didn't have to accept that kind of behavior from another human being.

- To divorce my first husband—I followed my gut. I had never really discovered who I was. I had always been who I thought everyone wanted me to be. I made the decision and was able to find me in the process.

- To file for a divorce from my children's father after twenty-four years of marriage—I had gone through breast cancer four years before and finally took to heart what my father taught about living your life not just going through the motions.

- To divorce my husband after thirty years because of the lack of future common goals and dreams after the children were grown.

- To divorce the father of my children after sixteen years of marriage (the oldest child was ten and the youngest was two) because I had the knowledge of what the consequences would be to my children if I continued to live with an abusive alcoholic.

- Get out of an abusive relationship—encouragement and support of friends and family that life would be okay and better. Granted, there were some scary, rough times in making that move, but I have survived and lived a better life for making that decision.

Addiction

- To admit to being an alcoholic and handle it by getting treatment and staying sober.

- Make life decisions for others

- Turn off mother's life support—she passed away in peace.

- Letting my mother know, it was time to let go.

- Stop radiation and chemo and letting my husband go.

- Whether or not to give my husband medication that might kill him.

- To let my daughter be taken off life support, considering what was in HER best interests, not mine.

- To allow my grandmother to die with dignity—conversations I had had with her previous to her becoming ill

- Putting my mother in a nursing home and understanding that I could not do it by myself.

- Stop life support on my mom, her chances of a normal life were slim to none.

- Telling the doctor not to operate on my dad after his second massive heart attack in two days. I knew that if he was not able to live life the way he had before surgery, being able to be out in the woods hunting or on the water fishing. If he would be confined to his bed the rest of his life, he would hate me. The doctor told me that his chances of having a normal life were slim to none. I knew Dad did not want a life hooked up to machines, as much as I wanted him here with me.

- Letting a neurosurgeon remove a hematoma from my son's brain.

- Moving father to healthcare facility.

- Moving my mother from the family home and not letting her drive with the support from a very kind, but direct doctor.

- I think the most difficult decision I ever had to make was whether to move my mother in with us—I prayed a lot. I have revisited that decision numerous times over the last seven years, and I reviewed my research and then thought again, and still came up with the same answer. Some decisions, even if they are the best one for us, are hard.

Personal Behavior Changes

- Every day I have to force myself not to help unless asked and then not to go overboard.

- To stop being so hard on myself.

- Asking for help.

- Forgiving my mother for an affair when I was a young child.

- Leaving the life I knew at thirty-four and getting married.

- To not do exactly what your parents want you to do—to make a decision that they are not always "right" in the decisions for your life.

- To speak to my father after fifteen years of him saying to others outside the family that he had no children—I was an only child.

- To not rush up to visit my mother on her dying day— that I was able to say all that I had needed to in the prior six months of regular visits, she knew all that I thought and felt about her and her dying, I was at peace with my mother.

- Forgiving my mother—I realized that if I did not forgive my mother for not loving me the way that I needed to be loved, I would continue to give my power to her and would continue to play the "blame" and "victim" cards. I finally learned to love myself without needing it from others.

- Going to a therapist when I clearly needed to.

- Breaking away from family influence.

- Forgiving someone who truly hurt me.

Relocating

- To move to Illinois, knowing that parents needed my help.

- Whether to move away from my family or stay close to home—I stayed because I like where I am.

- To move from Indiana to Montana—away from my family.

- To move back home.

- To move after thirty years in one area.

- Moving back to take over the family business.

- Deciding to go ahead and buy my own home.

Career / Work

- Making a career change that required a substantial pay cut and "downgrade" in career status.

- Going back to work.

- To change jobs to become a REALTOR®.

- Deciding what I wanted to do for a living after college. College does not prepare you for what to do afterward unless you pursue a specialized field of study.

- Leaving a job I liked and was good at due to an irrational boss.

- To leave the first company I worked for (ten and a half years) knowing I had the confidence that I could contribute more in another company in the training and development field rather than being downsized.

- Leaving a company that I had built from the ground up, but that had lost its integrity and focus.

- Going into business for myself—risky, uncertainty, hard work, very costly

- To take a job with the YMCA or to continue working with my dad

- To change careers making a third of what I formerly did—I just caved in.

- To leave my secure government job for real estate.

- Switch to a job that paid less money, remembering what was important in my life; my spouse and mental, and physical well being.

- Working while our children were little.

- Whether to leave self-employment in private practice of law.

- Quitting my job and starting my own engineering firm.

Children

- Having a baby at a young age.

- To give up on trying to have kids after three years when we were facing the option of in-vitro fertilization.

- What to do with an unplanned pregnancy.

- To carry a child that was destined to be deformed.

- Not to have children—always too much of a career person.

- To put a baby up for adoption by trying to look to the future for him.

- To have a child—my husband and I talked to a counselor to make sure we had talked through this type of commitment.

- Letting our wayward teenager go; we were in a battle of wills. A therapist said we had a fifty/fifty chance she would eventually live life based on the values she was raised with.

- Not bail out an adult child. It was a defining moment to allow a young adult to have the confidence to know that they could get through this or if not, starting over was an option.

- I had to kick my son out of the house because he was abusing drugs and disrespecting and disobeying rules with the hope I had that the "Tough Love" theory was right.

- Adopting children.

- To let one of my children live his life by envisioning five years from now.

- Allowing my children to experience negative consequences and pain from poor decisions they had made without intervening, knowing that I deserved to be treated better and needed to be respected.

- To report my daughter's marijuana.

- To let my daughter live her own life, and make her own decisions.

- Giving up custody of my son after legal battle.

Dealing with Death

- To keep going after the death of my four-month-old with the help of my four-year-old son because he kept reminding me that Easton was always beside me in spirit and that no matter what, he and all my family still needed me.

- Unexpected death of first husband and having to make related decisions and arrangements.
- Having to put down our dog after a car crash.
- To have my beloved cat of sixteen years put down.
- Putting down a pet with separation anxiety (and otherwise healthy and happy).

Dealing with Family

- Whether to sue a family member for theft.
- Tough love with my sister (to get her straightened out).
- Having to ask my parents for help, after I was an adult and out on my own.

Education

- Going back to college with young children to raise.
- Pursue college or raise a family
- The only one of six children and the first female to leave home to go off to college
- Returning to school for advanced degree.

■ What is the one thing you would do differently in your life?

Children

- I would not have had children.
- I would have adopted or fostered if I really felt a maternal need. I had children very young and I feel that I did

not allow myself time to get out into the world. God doesn't have a return policy.

- Try harder to have a child or more children.

- I cheated my son by not giving him brothers and sisters—a larger family makes for a close family.

- Build a kidney transplant house in my daughter, Crystal's, name—to keep her vibrant memory alive & to give back to those who helped her.

- Spend more time with my children instead of worrying about having a 'well-rounded' life.

- We're losing tradition, we don't eat together. The time you spend with your children defines who they will turn out to be. Understanding that family is the most important thing in the world—I passed the responsibility off to babysitters.

Would not have married

- Not get married so young; I needed more time to see who I am. My husband is very loving, but I still wonder what if....

- Two young people really had a hard time for ten long years—if we had been more mature we could have worked things out.

- I was expected to get married. I couldn't have the one I truly loved, so I settled for second best.

- I would follow my talents and dreams—know and celebrate the person I truly am.

- I was taught as a child to take care of others first! It is still a hard thing for me to put myself first, but I have become better at it the older I am. Unfortunately, at age sixty, my options are becoming less.

Divorce my Spouse

- Should have let my husband go years earlier, when he said that our marriage was a mistake, instead of years later after he moved us away from my family.

- Paying the price for it now, I'm not happy.

- He was not kind, respectful, or loving to me or our children.

- I didn't marry the right man; I should have married my high school sweetheart and lived the life I always thought I was going to have.

- Pursued my own life instead of marrying my first husband to get out of my parent's house. I was allowing someone else to control and make decisions for me instead of following my own heart.

- Should have attended or finished college

- For lifetime friends and perhaps a smoother path to my success

- To earn a better living, have a sense of achievement and be more confident

- To get a decent job; I'm too old now and cannot afford to go.

- I wouldn't have to worry now about retirement.

- I would be doing something that I had a passion for, not something I just fell into.

- Could have given me the courage to stand taller in my shoes.

- I believe I quit for two reasons: fear of failure and lack of focus. As a result I spent more years than I should have to become self-assured and have a sense of accomplishment.

- I would have stayed in school to become a nurse.

- At this stage of my life, education will be a tool to help me develop more skills for my profession or simply be for my own pleasure. I now take risks and will try something that may result in failure. I do not like failure but am no longer allowing it to restrict me.

- I have taken a back seat to raise my kids and put my children's dreams before mine.

- It is still very hard for women to get ahead in today's society and having a degree can at least increase a woman's chance of getting ahead.

- Because knowledge is power.

- Haven't gone back because it is too easy to put on a back burner.

- I have not returned to college because I read extensively and no longer feel it is necessary to have the cachet of 'diploma' to know that I know.

Take Better Care of my Health

- Never start smoking.

- Exercise throughout my life.

- Want to be active and alert into my retirement years.

- I want to enjoy a long healthy life to watch my grandchildren grow.

- I make excuses and am always so busy—Lack of discipline and time

- To not become an alcoholic—I wouldn't have said and done many hurtful things to others.

Saved More Money

- Invested when I was younger.

- I'm tired of being broke.

- To make sure I am able to support myself through retirement.

- Getting out of debt has been hard, but worth it.

- It's hard when it's expensive to live—so many of us live paycheck to paycheck.

- Invest money when I was younger—I would be able to give, travel, and relax more.

- I would have bought a home sooner and would never have gone into debt.

Changed my Behavior

- To offer more encouraging words, to those around you—words can either build people up or tear them down.

- Take more risks in general.

- Get rid of clutter—it complicates things.

- Smile more—there needs to be more humor and laughter in the world—too stressed.

- I wouldn't have stopped dancing growing up, dancing was the most important thing to me. As I got older, I had people tell me I couldn't be a dancer because of the way I looked. In college I took a couple classes and loved it, but couldn't see any future, so gave up. In my forties, I took a couple classes and was depressed by my body and the way it no longer responds to me. I can still picture and feel in my mind what it was like performing on stage (at my peak).

- Learn to accept and forgive myself for who I was at a much earlier age; wisdom comes with age but we need it so much sooner in life. That realization would have made my life so much easier and more enjoyable. Instead of trying to live up to certain standards or what I thought others wanted me to be, I would have been more comfortable in my skin, not tried to impress others or cared so much about what they thought I think. I am more "myself" now and I care less if others judge me. My new motto; be who you are and say what you feel, because those that matter don't mind and those that mind don't matter."

- Treated those that love me completely different—have more patience and understanding.

- I would not have depended on my husband so much. I stayed home and raised our children while he traveled all over the world building this wonderful career and now shares it with a woman my children's age.

- I want my family and friends to look at me the way they did before the divorce and cancer. I call it the sad eye.

Lived a Smaller, Simpler Life

- Stay true to my instincts—countless times they have been right but I didn't listen.

- Focused on myself more than everyone else—can't seem to find the balance I'm searching for.

- I would have moved out from my parents' home sooner and become independent, because all my life, I've "belonged" to someone. Now it's by choice. I love my husband and family, but I never took that chance to be free, because I was afraid—can't move out on my own.

There's that part of me that wishes I had my own place with nobody to answer to but myself.

- Be more proud of what I have accomplished and am accomplishing—having a strong self-worth and respect for oneself is the key to being able to give others the respect they deserve.

- I needed more patience. I think that it would have helped our son to make better decisions in his life.

- I have made some good choices and some bad ones, but I can only hope that I learned from all of the choices that I have made. It's important not to change because every experience and outcome has created who I am today.

- Things unfold as they do for a reason. I have appreciated all that I have experienced to date in my life and done so without regret and much gratitude.

- Even what I might call mistakes or missteps have been educational.

- I believe that every single second of my life has led to the place where I am right now. I am deeply, truly happy and would not change a thing because I am where I am because of my past decisions.

- I wouldn't change anything because I would not look the same, act the same, or have "my" unique character traits and beliefs that make me who I am.

Make a Career or Life Change

- Become an artist—I had talent, but was afraid! I use my talents for charities, I "get more" by giving.

- Less time working—more time to experience life and center on what is important.

- Explore alternative career options; discover my "passion" and get more satisfaction in work and life—fear, not a risk taker.

- I would become a writer—I have innate talent that pulls at me to use it—haven't moved on this due to lack of spousal support, economics, personal fear of failure, and personal fear of success.

- Work for myself—time and freedom of not having to answer to anyone else.

- Entered the education field earlier—I could have spent more time with the children and improved the quality of our home life—I teach now….with significantly greater debt but a greater quality of life.

- Volunteer more—for most of us, we will not have the opportunity to make a major impact on the world/masses, but it is life changing the impact we can make in small ways.

■ What are the top challenges you face in your work or career?

- Boredom due to the lack of creativity, challenges, and emotional rewards.

- Apathy of the unempowered that leads to employee retention issues

- Physical burnout—being underutilized, overqualified and unpaid for work done—sexual discrimination for equal pay.

- Co-worker issues relating to unaccountability, hidden agendas, and difficult personalities.

- Time management, organization, and life balance between career and home life.

- Finding the money in this economy for business growth and development—dealing with budget cuts and increasing costs of doing business.
- Lack of respect for my career abilities and competing in a male dominated environment.
- Developing positive management and leadership skills relating to motivation.
- Management transitions and skills
- Customer service, knowing how to handle issues professionally and earning the respect of our clients and communities we work with.
- Lack of effective communication and interoffice squabbling or gossip.
- Identifying positive change and then the lack of following through on great ideas and staying focused on what works.
- Lack of advancement within the company.
- Lack of confidence in myself.
- Keeping up with technology which may ultimately make my job obsolete.
- Not understanding how to market in our current environment.
- Lack of experience or education.
- Keeping up with law and occupational changes.
- Lack of qualified workers.
- Women not helping other women succeed or backstabbing.
- Generational differences.

■ What does it take to build a strong, positive work environment?

- Positive, respectful, appreciative, and encouraging involvement by managers.

- Open, honest communication and feedback.

- Hire positive people who are team players and thin the ranks of employees who are a negative influence.

- Strong uplifting leaders who support their employees by listening, having the courage to make and back up tough decisions, act with enthusiasm, and are fair in their treatment of employees.

- Self-discipline and excellent work ethic which in turn allows employees to take ownership of their position.

- Create a fun, upbeat environment.

- Provide opportunities for cooperation, collaboration, being engaged, and willingness to pitch in.

- Maintain a consistent management style—do what you say you will do and keep your word.

- Have strategic planning sessions and develop a vision for the future with defined goals and accountability to reach those goals.

- Allow and encourage creative freedom and risk taking.

- Work with each employee's strengths rather than focus on the negatives—praising people to success.

- Encourage all employees to continue learning and provide those opportunities.

- Shared ethics and values such as truthfulness and uncovering truth before action.

- Concentrate on work and leave the personal baggage or gossip at home.

- Always try your best at all that you do.

- Have transparency of management decisions so the employees understand and take ownership of the decisions that are made.

- Have an attitude of customer service in regard to the employees who work at the organization.

- Flexibility of management decisions to coincide with individual circumstances, when possible.

■ What do you believe destroys the culture of a business?

- Negative attitudes that include back biting, gossip, lack of teamwork, and not supporting the company effort.

- Deceit and dishonesty

- Self-centered behavior where every issue is "all about me", greed in all forms, and addiction to power.

- Lack of communication and understanding between management and employees—no communication that is positive, informative, and transparency of management regarding company issues.

- Office politics—favoritism—top down directives

- Lack of ambition by employees—apathy—not working up to potential—poor work ethic

- Caste system—lack of caring management—too many administrators

- Micro-managing employees—no room for people to be creative.

- Lack of respecting employees or each other—work against each other.

- Management not staying on top of what goes on with workers—limited commitment to employees

- Poor customer service.

- Inability to make decisions—inconsistent in carrying out decisions.

- Lack of company organization.

- Uninformed or "clueless" managers and supervisors, poor hiring practices, and wrong people in the different position.

- Sense of entitlement among employees who don't stop to think how their behaviors affect the goals, objectives, and bottom line of the company.

■ What do you rejoice in the most?

Personal / Family

- Family and friends

- Children's health, happiness and success

- Personal accomplishments, career growth

- Empowerment for women—capable, concerning, incredibly strong

- My job, getting new business, and paying bills

- My ability to impact so many lives.

- Volunteerism

- Vacation time

- In being heard

Life in General

- Everyday pleasures; miracles, laughter, food, friendship
- Being alive.
- Anything that works well and makes my life easier.
- The fact we have hope—we have the ability to alter mistakes and make changes for a brighter tomorrow.
- Uncertainty of life—new opportunities
- Watching a child experience something for the first time.

Religion / Spirituality

- Belief that God is with me and leads my life.
- The power of our Lord and Savior, Jesus Christ, our salvation
- The spiritual awakening that is happening.
- Spirituality and love for most of mankind
- A generation that will serve God.

Government / Liberties

- Freedom of religion, choice, speech, and expression
- Personal opportunities to grow and thrive
- Right of ownership

Culture / People in General

- Global and local community
- People who live for and beyond a higher purpose and have found their calling.
- There is still love and connectedness, one on one.

- How people with means are reaching out to those in need and to stop violence.

- The sense of service to others that I see in most people.

- The connections that can be made between people when time is taken to really listen.

- Kindness in the world, if we are willing to look.

- The great intelligence of the younger generations.

- Raising kind, caring, giving, loving, and productive members of society.

- Faith in people and the love, appreciation, humor, and respect I have for myself.

- Ability to travel and see other parts of the world.

Technology

- Our amazing technology and opportunities.

- Internet that enables us to correspond so easily and inexpensively with family and friends throughout the globe—tapping into the wealth of information on the Internet.

Characteristics

- Unconditional love

- Laughter

- Gratitude

- Positive, comfortable people

- Common sense held by individuals

- Intelligence and connectivity

- The spirit of many of our citizens

■ What do you wish to have happen for your children?

- Love life and live it to the fullest and have a Christ centered life.

- The next eight years, get them through high school and college—then a successful life and careers.

- Career wise: I want them to do what they have passion for. Something they can wake up to every morning and say "I can't wait to go to work."

- I want my kids to make wise decisions in their lives— to be hardworking, kind, and respectful. I truly believe if they can do this, they will be successes in life and will live happy, prosperous lives. Of course, good decisions means choosing an educational path that will help them achieve their professional desires, they will choose to be with people who treat them well and bring them joy, and they will avoid drugs, alcohol, and the poisons of life that get people de-railed.

- If I have them? I want them to be content.

- If I ever have them, for them to lead happy lives.

- That she will serve God in all that she does.

- Happiness in family and fulfillment in career

- Long, happy, satisfying life doing what they want to do.

- That they have a quality spiritual life, meaningful work, and relationships.

- I wish each of my children to have a personal relationship with Jesus Christ and to know they can work for anything their hearts desire.

- They are both highly talented, creative people, and I hope they can find a way to be successful in their life's work, doing what they love.

- Find a soul mate and financial security.

- I hope my daughter truly follows her passion of being an artist because one should go thru life doing what they love. Of course, I have also told her to get another degree in a career that pays well until the artist thing gets off the ground.

- That they would fulfill Gods purpose for them.

- Good health would be a blessing.

- That they grow up healthy and happy.

- That they are whole.

- For them to be happy and successful.

- For his dreams to come true.

- For both of them to find the right life partner.

- Stability

- I wish for them to have everything they need and some of what they want, both spiritually and materially.

- Happiness and success

- That they have loving families and are happy.

- For my twenty-six-year-old son to realize he can have a very positive influence on this world if he just applies himself.

- Have unconditional love with spouse, good health, and financial security.

- If I had children, I would want them to enjoy the simple pleasures of life…watching a garden grow, playing in the sprinklers, sledding for hours. As adults we forgot these simple things. I want my children to have strong educational values and learn at their own pace… not have "No child left behind" results jammed down their throats.

- Their dreams and desires are achieved. Making choices and sacrifices necessary for them to realize their dreams.
- A healthy and happy marriage.
- That they grow up happy and healthy and that they find something they are passionate about that can also support them.
- To live a happy, healthy, fulfilling life.
- Children
- Be happy and leave the world better than he found it.
- I want them to be happy and spend lots of time laughing.
- Happiness
- I am fortunate enough to be seeing that, both graduated college, have wonderful jobs, my son is married, but my daughter has a definite distrust of men since the divorce so I wish her healing.
- Happiness
- To always put the Lord first, and live, laugh and most importantly LOVE!
- Rewarding careers and satisfying relationships
- I want my daughter to grow up in a traditional family and enjoy her childhood. I want her to graduate from college and have a career she enjoys. I hope she has a family of her own and is a better mother than I am and is able to balance her career and her family.
- Find a lifelong mate!
- Continue to have the best opportunities to learn and develop into a wonderful person.

- That she lives a long, happy life doing exactly what she wants to do.

- I just want them to happy and content with their lives.

- For them to be sold out one hundred percent to God— His will, His way, His word.

- More open society

- Peace with themselves—Comfortable in their own skins.

- I want to be instrumental in making sure that they are one of the ones who "get it" (nieces, nephews in my case).

- Less hatred and fear of those who speak a different language or practice a different religion.

- I wish for my daughter to travel and decide where she wants to be for herself. I would love for her to find herself before she finds someone that will stifle her passions. Or before she stifles her passions to conform to what someone else wants. I wish her to have a better easier life than I have had.

- That she would have lived past thirty-three years.

- Good health and financial success

- Health, happiness first—and enough success but not too much.

- That they are happy, prosperous, and have a purpose that is greater than themselves.

- That I win the lottery so I can help them out. Ummm, wait, that's too easy. That they be healthy, happy, productive members of society. Not doing too well so far.

- That they become self-sufficient and satisfied in their life choices.

- That they may make a decent living and happiness.

- I wish my girls would have the ability to get a great education and do something that would change their life as well as someone else.

- They have contentment.

- They have an easier better life than me.

- Be happy.

- She will be happy in her chosen career, love, and laughter.

- Unconditional love, every success reached for, pride and fulfillment in life

- Our two girls are very successful financially and have wonderful families.

- That they have healthy, happy lives.

- I wish them all the happiness the world has to offer. And that they are respectable adults.

- If I had children, I would want them to be healthy and happy.

- Continued happiness and success.

- Self-knowledge, self-acceptance, personal goals, doing for others, contentment

- I would like them to be productive citizens, doing what they enjoy and hopefully sustaining themselves with their choice.

- That they can be happy in whatever they choose to do as their life's work.

- I wish my children were all active Christians and fulfilled in their career and personal life.

- Health, happiness and wealth (in that order)

- My hope is that he finds his soul mate and a career that is fulfilling. I hope that he is ever so happy and experiences health and prosperity.

- That they set goals for themselves, know they will fail at things but get back up and try again at that or something new, and always believe in themselves. Yhe self-confidence in yourself will allow you to dream the dreams and make them come true.

- I wish my children to take risks, embrace the pain as well as the joy, and know that every experience is a piece of the puzzle that makes them unique. I wish for them to have incredible insight into the "whys" of life.

- I wish my children to find joy and happiness in their jobs and families and friends!

- I want them to be happy and healthy. I want them to be able to take up for those who cannot take up for themselves.

- I want them to feel fulfilled in every way possible.

- Lifestyle and career choices—I want them to be happy (not necessarily rich, but that would be okay too).

- That they are contributing members of society, that they are good parents, grown children, neighbors and friends. That they find peace and happiness in their lives.

- A friendlier world

- That they are happy, healthy and financially intelligent—take care of themselves.

- High education

- I have twenty-one nieces and nephews who are like my own. My wish for them to honor all work and respect for themselves as people, and to appreciate their family, who they are, and to affirm their own gifts to bring to the world making a positive difference…

- Happiness, the gift of true love and education that I never received.

- College of their choice, anywhere and money not be a concern.

- For any child (since I don't have my own)—the best thing I can wish for them all is to have someone in their life who instills in them a sense of pride/self-respect. Without that, nothing else matters.

- I want them to be independent, successful, contribute to the betterment of our community and to be happy.

- Love life, be respected, be good people

- For them to be happy, healthy doing work they enjoy with partners who respect them.

- A clear path to happiness and self-fulfillment.

- I want my kids to grow up happy and feeling loved and safe and secure. I want them to grow up knowing how much I loved them and do love them and will always love them no matter what. I also hope that my kids will end up happy and content with their life and will always remember to be thankful to God for all that he has blessed them with.

- Have a happy childhood that protects them from becoming adults too soon.

- I have step children, wish them health, wealth, and a happy life.

- A good and happy life.

- Use their talents/gifts and be near God.

- Would like them to pursue higher education and fulfill their true potentials in addition, would like them to meet and have healthy, loving and satisfying relationships with members of the opposite sex.

- Success, happiness

- Continue in happy and prosperous marriage relationships. Nurture their children.

- Happiness, love, and peace with what they choose to do with their lives.

- Happiness and success in personal life—security.

- I want them to lead full, happy lives (careers and personal).

- To grow up to be able to live their dreams and to be happy.

- Happiness and health

- Happiness, fulfillment, marriage, children, health, financial stability

- I want them to take their gifts and change lives for the positive.

- I wish for them to grow up with a strong love for one another.

- That they remain true to their natures and continue to be a blessing to those they serve.

- Peace and prosperity, as well as good health.

- I don't have any kids. I have two step-grandchildren, to be comfortable with themselves.

- I want them to be happy, enjoy raising their children, and have successful careers.
- To find love and happiness and someone to share that with.
- That they have happy, fruitful lives.
- For my nephew, I hope that he gets insurance and doesn't hurt himself on his job.
- Enjoy life and finish school (I don't have children yet, but that is what I want for them).
- That they treasure each day of their life with its joys and tribulations.
- That they never encounter anything other than life's most awesome treasures.
- They can be happy in their lives.
- They succeed in whatever they want to do and they are happy in life.
- To know joy in their lives. To be great parents. To enjoy their loved ones.
- My biggest wish for my child is that he overcomes his autism/development delay. I want him to experience life as a 'normal' child.
- To be happy.
- My youngest is close to graduating from college, I wish for her to find "the perfect job" where she feels fulfilled.
- Excellent health, security, faith in self that all things are possible
- That they be happy and always feel loved.
- That he is happy and fulfilled with his choices and makes a contribution to society through his life.

- That they will healthy, happy, and reach their full potential.
- They live the life that makes them happy.
- For them to discover their most meaningful purpose in life whatever that may be for them.
- Live happily independent of me.
- Total happiness and freedom
- That they become responsible, hard-working contributors that are accountable and responsible.
- I wish them the wisdom and strength to face life's challenges and the bumps in the road with faith and perseverance.
- I would like to see my children achieve financial success.
- Know Christ, become educated on financial matters, and guard their heart, ears, eyes, and mind against evil temptations.
- Fall in love, have a family, and a career they enjoy.
- Long healthy, adventurous, happy lives

■ What are the top life lessons women would benefit from knowing?

- Don't be a martyr for your children; it weakens your self-worth.
- Never take your family for granted.
- The man you marry may be your prince charming; however he may not have the prince's bank account.

- Don't settle for less than what you want. Once you do it takes a lot of time and energy to make up for it.
- Don't take it personal.
- Don't fool yourself; be what you are.
- Keep good notes.
- You must have humor; it will get you through kids, marriage, menopause and dealing with workplace issues.
- Don't be afraid of being alone.
- You will survive your teenagers even if it doesn't seem like it.
- Respect yourself first and learn to trust your feelings.
- Be honest to yourself.
- You can't please everyone.
- Follow your heart and dreams.
- Stay connected to God.
- Women have amazing inner-self strength.
- Compromise is not taking second place.
- Don't stay with a man who is abusing you.
- It can take years to build up trust, but only seconds to destroy it.
- Embrace change without whining.
- The truth will set you free, but first it will shatter the safe, sweet way you live.
- Lead with kindness.
- Act as if you face no barriers as a woman. I was too stupid to realize that non-traditional careers were not

available to me and as a result I managed to find a reserve unit in the seventies that sent women to the field. I entered electronic technical training in the eighties and as a young girl was the only female that was invited to play "street" football with the boys. Somebody forgot to tell me that I should not take on traditional male roles. I was lucky and found a place within the "man's" world without fighting. I know that this is partly tremendous luck. I have to believe that the fact that I naturally gravitated toward people that did not consider gender and that it was partly because I did not realize the obstacle was there and acted as if I belonged in this circle.

- Do not live your life for others.

- Women can do anything they want—they even can be President.

- Always tell the people you love that you love them.

- Be true to your own beliefs, not what others believe to be true about you.

- You are special—God doesn't make any junk.

- Harboring anger is a waste of time and energy; learn to forgive others.

- That it's okay to show emotion.

- Be very choosy about your mate.

- Get the highest education.

- Decide early in life what you want for yourself and go for it.

- It is not your fault if your partner abuses you; it is their need for power and control.

- Do it right the first time—you don't get a second chance to make a first impression.

- There's no such thing as "perfect"—it's an illusion.

- Separate the person from the issue.

- Try to work out problems early, they just get worse.

- You can't change people—it's a mistake to think you can or to try.

- Everything is relative; if a problem seems insurmountable at the moment, think if and how it will affect your life.

- Be yourself, yet be aware of the needs of others.

- Talk to peers about investments.

- Don't rush into marriage.

- Go to school and get your degree and never let anyone tell you you're not smart enough.

- Don't quit, obstacles are just another way to toughen your skills.

- Learn from your mistakes.

- Stay close to your girlfriends; men often come and go, parents die, we don't all have sisters that are so like us, we would choose them as friends; your girlfriends can last a lifetime and often do, and they will be there when no one else will.

- You can change your day, by changing your mind.

- Trust your instinct.

- Everything happens for a reason.

- You don't need a man to survive.

- Attitude is everything.

- Have fun with your children, the work will wait.
- Supermom will crash and burn if not cared for.
- Be your own boss.
- If you chose to be a stay at home mom, make sure you maintain your skills and network.
- Don't let fear dictate your future. Try something new.
- Don't settle for second best.
- Never doubt your intuition and the strength of your inner voice.
- Sometimes it is okay to do nothing and wait to observe the situation.
- Marriage should be a partnership.
- Surround yourself with people smarter than you are.
- Live again after rape.
- Have self-respect.
- Seek first to understand (before "assuming").
- Study and talk to experts before you make an important decision.
- The answer is always no, if you don't ask!
- If you want something done right- do it yourself.
- We are our own worst enemy.
- You can do just about anything you want to do.
- Always protect your heart but be willing to love someone unconditionally.
- It's not a bad thing to want money.
- Just because you are a woman does not mean that you can't do a male dominate job.

- Nurture yourself each day—you cannot take care of anyone else unless you first take care of yourself.
- Listen to your intuition.
- Just keep doing what is right and it will pay off.
- Be confident and independent.
- Get help and support, you can't do it alone.
- Have fun, life is too short to worry about the small stuff.
- We are each responsible for ourselves.
- You must love yourself, before you can allow others to love you.
- Never say never.
- Take responsibility for your life and happiness.
- Marriage is a gift, not a right.
- Follow your heart no matter what.
- Never give of yourself too freely.
- Plan ahead for your own future.
- Life is a banquet—don't starve!
- Find God's purpose for you.
- Not making a decision to do something is a decision itself.
- Trust someone until they give you a reason not to.
- Live for the moment.
- We don't need to sacrifice time with our family to be successful in business.
- Always admit to your mistakes.
- Don't ignore the "elephant" in the room.

- Keep an eye on your back side.

- If a man is spending most of the time looking at your boobs during a conversation, he is really not worth it.

- Choose not to believe people are discriminating against you.

- Pretty is superficial, beauty is rooted in the soul, only those that matter can see beauty.

- Get some financial security: a life insurance policy on your spouse, a bank account.

- Live each day as if it is your last.

- Allow yourself to be happy and enjoy all the wonders around you.

- Remember we are all connected—be compassionate.

- When you are a size eight, you are not fat! Now that I'm a size sixteen, I wish I would have spent more time enjoying when I was a size eight.

- Everyone won't like you.

- Save your money.

- Lead by example.

- Women can learn from men and men can learn from women.

- Everything happens for a reason and someday you will come to understand that reason.

- You have to learn to control your attitude or it will control you.

- Forgive.

- The world is not fair—Pick one cause to fight for or a charity and give your heart and soul to change something.

- It is okay to leave dirty dishes in the sink until the next morning and read a bedtime story.

- When you lose a spouse to death you never "get over" that love, you simply learn to live with the memories.

- There's always a chance for a more satisfactory childhood—you reframe and relive it in your mind.

- Babies are never bad news—maybe bad timing, but never bad news.

- Choose your battles.

- Trust your abilities.

- Travel, see the world and have the time of your life, and do the "me" things before you become a wife.

- Take the knowledge of co-workers and use it to your advantage.

- Speak up for yourself.

- Never get on top after you're forty. (Sorry, it had to be said).

- Always keep your word.

- Never stay in a relationship that's toxic, whether a friendship or romantic.

- Common sense is more important and will get you further than a degree.

- Someone else can always do your job, no one is irreplaceable.

- Listen to your parents when choosing a life partner.

- You don't always learn the best lessons from successful projects. It is the failures that you learn from.

- Realize that out of controversy there is always opportunity.

- It is often rare that one can choose how they die, but you can certainly choose how you live.

- Set your standards high when considering a spouse… and…Don't 'do' sex, until you say 'I do'!

- Never get angry in public, always try to keep your cool until you are alone. Buy a punching bag.

- Live simply. It's very freeing!

- No man defines who a woman is!

- Not everyone will be happy for you if you "succeed."

- Find your own way, before you try to lead others.

- Life will never be in complete balance, yet stay on the teeter-totter.

- Try to learn something new each day—learning is forever.

- You aren't the only one going through whatever you are going through.

- Be a mentor to younger women.

- Make your life an adventure so you can always smile when you look back on it.

- Do not judge others until you get to know them.

- Practice tough love when necessary.

- You are not your past; you can create your future.

- Life is not measured by the number of breaths we take, but by the moments that take our breath away.

- Being a mother is a true blessing, not a right.

- Give credit to those who helped you get things done.

- Treat people nice, but don't get stepped on.

- Keep close to your friends and continue to make new ones.

- Be yourself—don't let people intimidate you into hiding your true colors.

- Smile—it's the cheapest thing you have that you can give others.

- Be loyal to other women.

- Be the change you seek!

- Be tenacious.

- Look at what you can fix—what is your part in the situation.

- Choose a career that will give you personal satisfaction and don't be afraid to change the definition or direction.

- Don't burn any bridges.

- Utilize your intuition; it is what gets you out of the messes you might come up against in life or even keep you from getting yourself in a mess in the first place.

- It's okay to be a stay at home mom.

- Making yourself happy is better for your family than anything else.

- Be a global citizen.

- Be passionate about life and teach your children to be.

- Do the right thing because it's the right thing to do no matter how uncomfortable it makes you feel.

- Accept your accomplishments.

- Work is work…not your whole life.

- Your husband can be your best friend.

- Given enough time, a fraud will expose itself.

- When you have been knocked flat over and over, it is up to you to find the strength to get up once again.

- Believe in miracles.

- No one can save you but you.

- Don't seek emotional approval.

- Learn to communicate and work with all generations especially with the changing workforce.

- Listen more, ask more questions than answers.

- You don't have to always be strong.

- Choose to work only with people you like and respect.

- You will find joy in something if you are willing to look for it.

- Just because a woman is aggressive or strong doesn't mean she is a bitch.

- Relationships are more important than things.

- Do something for someone else each day.

- You can be strong even if you think you are weak; fake it and eventually you will be strong.

- Disagreeing in a calm, rational fashion is so much more effective than throwing tantrums, and folks I've treated with respect in the past have often become unanticipated allies on future projects. Even though burning that bridge might be satisfying in the short term, beware of long term implications and plan your words carefully.

- Learn to summarize your comments; learn to speak in an adult voice.

- Never let the noise around you get in the way of what you are trying to accomplish.
- Be a good friend.
- Give yourself a break when you are not up to your high standards.
- Don't gossip.
- Be happy at your job. "Bloom where you are planted."
- Find the positive in every situation—even the bad ones.
- Practice random acts of kindness every day.
- Not everyone wants you to be self-sufficient.
- Stop comparing yourself to others, compete against yourself, be better today than you were yesterday.
- Learn from others; everyone is in the same boat in one way or another.
- Do not talk about your children all the time.
- Fight the battles you can win.
- Every person has a story and a lesson to tell, listen more, and try to understand.
- Be good to your parents; they aren't here forever.
- Be creative—it's not hard to think outside the box once you get started.
- Believe in yourself and others will believe in you, too.
- Surround yourself with strong, caring, supportive people.
- Don't put yourself in a position to get yourself in trouble.
- Try to learn how to fix some of the things that might go wrong in your house.

- Enjoy your life because you only get this one chance to leave a happy legacy.

- If you really want something, you better make up your mind to go after it, because it won't just happen by itself.

- Don't live with regrets.

- Fill your mind with positive self-talk.

About the Author

Karel Murray, CSP

Karel brings meaning to mayhem with her "nothing but the truth" approach to business and life. An accomplished author and humorist, Karel has made radio and television appearances and she enjoys local, regional, and national publication of her articles. In addition to *Hitting Our Stride: Women, Work and What Matters*, she is the author of *Straight Talk: Getting Off the Curb*. Karel is a featured author in *Extreme Excellence: Dynamic Interviews with America's Top 10 Performance Experts*, and publishes a monthly newsletter—*Think Forward!*® read by thousands of subscribers. She is author of both *The Profitability Blueprint Series*® and the *CPR for Managers Series* and has created a weekly podcast series where she interviews industry experts on various topics: http://www.JustForAMomentPodcast.com.

Karel holds a BA in Human Resources and has earned numerous designations and certifications, including the prestigious National Speakers Association CSP (Certified Speaking Professional) and the Real Estate Educators Association DREI (Distinguished Real Estate Instructor). Her resume includes experience as a human resources regional executive of a large commercial insurance firm, as an award-winning sales person, as a manager of a top producing real estate office, and now as owner of Our Branch, Inc., a national and international speaking and training company.

She has received several awards for her community service, including the Blue Springs Missouri Chamber of Commerce Award, and once taught a pig named Nelson to jump rope… but that's another story.

She is a member of the National Speakers Association and a Board Director for the Minnesota NSA Chapter, Meeting Professionals International and has served as a Board of Director member and officer for the National Real Estate Educators Association. As a professional keynote speaker, Karel has had the pleasure of connecting with hundreds of audiences throughout the US and abroad.

When not on the road, Karel can be found in Waterloo, Iowa, with her ever wonderfully patient husband Rick and their attentive brood of four—at last head count—cats and dogs.

CPSIA information can be obtained
at www.ICGtesting.com
Printed in the USA
FFOW01n1533200516
24172FF